enVision® Algebra 2

Common Core
Standards Practice
Workbook

Copyright © 2024 by Savvas Learning Company LLC. All Rights Reserved. Printed in the United States of America.

This publication is protected by copyright, and permission should be obtained from the publisher prior to any prohibited reproduction, storage in a retrieval system, or transmission in any form or by any means, electronic, mechanical, photocopying, recording, or otherwise. For information regarding permissions, request forms, and the appropriate contacts within the Savvas Learning Company Rights Management group, please send your query to the address below.

Savvas Learning Company LLC, 15 East Midland Avenue, Paramus, NJ 07652

Common Core State Standards: Copyright © 2010. National Governors Association Center for Best Practices and Council of Chief State School Officers. All rights reserved.

Savvas® and **Savvas Learning Company®** are the exclusive trademarks of Savvas Learning Company LLC in the U.S. and other countries.

Savvas Learning Company publishes through its famous imprints **Prentice Hall®** and **Scott Foresman®** which are exclusive registered trademarks owned by Savvas Learning Company LLC in the U.S. and/or other countries.

Other Savvas trademarks such as **enVision®** and **Savvas Realize™** are exclusive trademarks of Savvas Learning Company LLC in the U.S. and/or other countries.

Unless otherwise indicated herein, any third party trademarks that may appear in this work are the property of their respective owners, and any references to third party trademarks, logos, or other trade dress are for demonstrative or descriptive purposes only. Such references are not intended to imply any sponsorship, endorsement, authorization, or promotion of Savvas Learning Company products by the owners of such marks, or any relationship between the owner and Savvas Learning Company LLC or its authors, licensees, or distributors.

ISBN-13: 978-1-418-40226-6
ISBN-10:   1-418-40226-5

Contents

enVision® Algebra 2

Common Core Standards Practice

EOC Practice Test Form A

EOC Practice Test Form B

Mathematics Reference Sheet

Common Core Standards Practice

HSN.CN.A.1, HSN.CN.A.2

1. Simplify the expression.
   $(8 + 2i) - (3 - i)$
   - Ⓐ $11 + i$
   - Ⓑ $7 - i$
   - Ⓒ $5 + i$
   - Ⓓ $5 + 3i$

2. Simplify the expression $(4i - 1)^2$.
   - Ⓐ $-17 - 8i$
   - Ⓑ $-15 - 8i$
   - Ⓒ $15 - 8i$
   - Ⓓ $17 - 8i$

3. Simplify the expression.
   $2i(3 + 5i)(3 - 5i)$

4. Simplify the expression.
   $2(i - 8) + (3 - 5i)$
   Write the solution in the form $a + bi$.

5. Simplify the expression $\frac{4 + i}{2 - i}$.
   - Ⓐ $-1.4 - 1.2i$
   - Ⓑ $-1.4 + 1.2i$
   - Ⓒ $1.4 - 1.2i$
   - Ⓓ $1.4 + 1.2i$

6. Write the product $(2i - 6)(4 + 3i)$ in the form $a + bi$.
   - Ⓐ $30 - 10i$
   - Ⓑ $-18 + 18i$
   - Ⓒ $-30 - 10i$
   - Ⓓ $-24 + 4i$

7. Which of the following is a complex factorization of 61?
   - Ⓐ $(6 - 5i)(6 + 5i)$
   - Ⓑ $(6 - 5i)^2$
   - Ⓒ $2(3 - 5i)(3 + 5i)$
   - Ⓓ $(6 + 5i)^2$

8. Simplify the expression
   $i(3 - 4i) - (i + 5)$.
   Write the solution in the form $a + bi$.

9. Callie simplified $\frac{6 + 2i}{1 + 2i}$ and wrote her answer in the form $a + bi$. What is the value of $a + b$?

10. Which of the following expressions are equivalent to 1? Select all that apply.

- ☐ A. i^4
- ☐ B. i^{10}
- ☐ C. i^{18}
- ☐ D. i^{24}
- ☐ E. i^{32}
- ☐ F. i^{46}

11. Simplify the expression.
$(3i - 2)(6 - 2i)$

Ⓐ $-18 + 14i$
Ⓑ $-6 + 22i$
Ⓒ $6 + 22i$
Ⓓ $18 + 14i$

12. Which factor should you multiply the fraction by to simplify the expression $\frac{6-i}{3+i}$?

Ⓐ $\frac{3+i}{3+i}$
Ⓑ $\frac{6+i}{6+i}$
Ⓒ $\frac{3-i}{3-i}$
Ⓓ $\frac{6-i}{6-i}$

13. Simplify the expression.
$i(3 - i)(2 + 5i)$

Write the solution in the form $a + bi$.

14. Simplify the expression.
$(3 + 4i) + (8 + 7i)$

Ⓐ $-5 - 3i$
Ⓑ $7 + 15i$
Ⓒ $11 + 11i$
Ⓓ $15 + 7i$

15. Simplify the expression.
$2i(6 - i)(6 + i)$

Ⓐ $-24 + 70i$
Ⓑ $24 + 70i$
Ⓒ 74
Ⓓ $74i$

16. Select True or False for each statement.

Statement	True	False
The sum of two complex numbers is always a complex number.	☐	☐
The difference of two complex numbers is always a complex number.	☐	☐
The product of two complex numbers is always a complex number.	☐	☐
The quotient of two complex numbers is always a complex number.	☐	☐

Name _____

Common Core Standards Practice

HSN.CN.C.7, HSN.CN.C.8, HSN.CN.C.9

1. Which describes the solutions to the equation $x^2 + 2x + 16 = 0$?
   - (A) two rational roots
   - (B) two irrational roots
   - (C) two complex imaginary roots
   - (D) one double root

2. Which describes the solutions to the equation $3x^2 + 10x = 9$?
   - (A) two rational roots
   - (B) two irrational roots
   - (C) two complex imaginary roots
   - (D) one double root

3. Which equation has complex roots with imaginary parts?
   - (A) $2x^2 + 5x - 4 = 0$
   - (B) $4x^2 - 7x + 9 = 0$
   - (C) $3x^2 - 6x + 1 = 0$
   - (D) $x^2 - 8x - 20 = 0$

4. What are the solutions to the equation $x^2 + 4x + 5 = 0$? Select all solutions.
   - ☐ A. -5
   - ☐ B. -1
   - ☐ C. 1
   - ☐ D. 5
   - ☐ E. $-2 + i$
   - ☐ F. $-2 - i$

5. What are the solutions to the equation $10x^2 - 8x - 6 = 0$?
   - (A) $\dfrac{-2 \pm i\sqrt{11}}{5}$
   - (B) $\dfrac{-2 \pm \sqrt{19}}{5}$
   - (C) $\dfrac{-2 \pm i\sqrt{11}}{5}$
   - (D) $\dfrac{2 \pm \sqrt{19}}{5}$

6. Which equation has two real solutions?
   - (A) $-9x - 5 = 3x^2$
   - (B) $5x^2 + 2 = 2x$
   - (C) $x^2 + 8x = -24$
   - (D) $2x^2 = x - 9$

7. Which are the solutions to the equation $x^2 + 23 = 8x$?
   - (A) $-4 \pm i\sqrt{7}$
   - (B) $4 \pm i\sqrt{7}$
   - (C) $-4 \pm \sqrt{39}$
   - (D) $4 \pm \sqrt{39}$

8. Francisco solved the quadratic equation $3x^2 - 7x + 5 = 0$.

$$x = \frac{7 - \sqrt{49 - 4(3)(5)}}{2(3)}$$

$$x = \frac{7 - \sqrt{49 - 60}}{6}$$

$$x = \frac{7 - \sqrt{-11}}{6}$$

$$x = \frac{7 + \sqrt{11}}{6}$$

Is he correct? Choose the best explanation.

Ⓐ Francisco is correct; he used the quadratic formula and substituted numbers correctly and simplified the expression.

Ⓑ Francisco is not correct; he should have written $-\sqrt{-11}$ as $-i\sqrt{11}$ instead of $+\sqrt{11}$.

Ⓒ Francisco is not correct; the − in the numerator of the original expression should be a ±, but otherwise he solved correctly.

Ⓓ Francisco is not correct; the − in the numerator of the original expression should be a ±, and he should have written $\sqrt{-11}$ as $i\sqrt{11}$ instead of the opposite of $\sqrt{11}$.

9. Which are the solutions to the equation $x^2 - 7x + 13 = 0$?

Ⓐ $\dfrac{-7 \pm i\sqrt{3}}{2}$

Ⓑ $\dfrac{-7 \pm \sqrt{101}}{2}$

Ⓒ $\dfrac{7 \pm i\sqrt{3}}{2}$

Ⓓ $\dfrac{7 \pm \sqrt{101}}{2}$

10. How many roots does the equation $ax^2 = bx + c$, where a, b, and c are integers, have in the complex number system?

Ⓐ exactly 0 roots

Ⓑ exactly 2 unique roots

Ⓒ exactly 2 roots including repeated roots

Ⓓ either 2 roots or 0 roots

Common Core Standards Practice

HSA.SSE.A.1.a, HSA.SSE.A.1.b

1. What are the x-intercepts of the function $y = 3(x - 6)(x + 5)$? Select all that apply.
   - ☐ A. –6
   - ☐ B. –5
   - ☐ C. 3
   - ☐ D. 5
   - ☐ E. 6

2. What is the value of the constant in the expression?
   $2x - 5x^3 + 7 - 6x^2$
   - Ⓐ –6
   - Ⓑ –5
   - Ⓒ 2
   - Ⓓ 7

3. The function $A(t) = 500(1 + 0.06)^t$, models the value of an account A as a function of years t, as it grows with a fixed annual interest. What does the expression (1 + 0.06) represent?
   - Ⓐ Each year the account grows by $1.06.
   - Ⓑ At the end of each year the account is worth 106% of what it was worth the previous year.
   - Ⓒ Each year the value of the account will grow by 106%.
   - Ⓓ In the initial amount or principal in the account was $1.06.

4. What is the coefficient of the x-term in the equation?
   $y = 2x^3 + 8 - x + 2x^2$

5. The area of a rectangular painting is $12x^2 + 11x - 15$ square feet. Which of the following could be the dimensions of the painting?
   - Ⓐ $(4x - 3)$ feet by $(3x + 5)$ feet
   - Ⓑ $(4x + 3)$ feet by $(3x - 5)$ feet
   - Ⓒ $(12x - 3)$ feet by $(x + 5)$ feet
   - Ⓓ $(6x - 5)$ feet by $(2x + 3)$ feet

6. What does each number represent in the equation?
   $y = 3(x - 5)^2 + 4$

	3	4	5
y-intercept	☐	☐	☐
horizontal shift	☐	☐	☐
vertical shift	☐	☐	☐
vertical stretch	☐	☐	☐
x-intercept	☐	☐	☐

7. A rectangular garden has an area that can be represented by the polynomial $3x^2 - 16x - 64$. Which of the following represent the side lengths of the garden? Select all side lengths.
   - ☐ A. $x + 8$
   - ☐ B. $x - 8$
   - ☐ C. $8x + 3$
   - ☐ D. $3x + 8$
   - ☐ E. $3x - 8$

8. A rectangular piece of cardboard measures 20 cm by 32 cm. Barry cuts off some of the cardboard to make a new rectangular piece. The area of the new piece is represented by the expression $(20 - 2x)(32 - 2x)$. What does x represent?

   Ⓐ the width of cardboard, in centimeters, that Barry cuts from each of the 4 sides of the rectangle

   Ⓑ the width of cardboard, in centimeters, that is removed from the length and the width of the rectangle

   Ⓒ the total area of cardboard, in square centimeters, that Barry cuts off the rectangle

   Ⓓ the area, in square centimeters, of each of the 4 pieces of cardboard that Barry cuts off the rectangle

9. The volume of a box is represented by the polynomial $x^3 - 10x^2 + 24x$. Which of the following represent the side lengths of the box? Select all side lengths.

   ☐ A. x
   ☐ B. $x - 4$
   ☐ C. $x + 4$
   ☐ D. $x - 6$
   ☐ E. $x + 6$

10. The height, in feet, of an acorn falling from a tree can be modeled by the equation $y = 46 - 16x^2$, where x is the time, in seconds, since the acorn started to fall. What does the value of 46 represent in the equation?

    Ⓐ the time, in seconds, for the acorn to fall to the ground

    Ⓑ the height, in feet, of the acorn before it started to fall

    Ⓒ the speed, in feet per second, of the acorn as it hits the ground

    Ⓓ the increase in the speed, in feet per second, during the first second that the acorn falls

11. A local wildlife group sometimes adds fish to lakes. The population of fish in one lake is modeled by the function $P(x) = 1.2x^3 - 8x^2 - x + 200$, where x is the number of years after 2020. What does the value 200 represent in the function?

    Ⓐ the annual increase in the number of fish in the lake

    Ⓑ the number of fish added to the lake each year by the wildlife group

    Ⓒ the number of fish in the lake in the year 2020

    Ⓓ the number of fish in the lake in the year 2220

Name _____

Common Core Standards Practice

HSA.SSE.A.2, HAS.SSE.B.4

1. Which expressions are equivalent to $16x^4 - 81y^4$? Select all that apply.
- ☐ A. $(4x^2 - 9y^2)^2$
- ☐ B. $(4x^2 - 9y^2)(4x^2 + 9y^2)$
- ☐ C. $(2x - 3y)(2x + 3y)^3$
- ☐ D. $(2x - 3y)^2(2x + 3y)^2$
- ☐ E. $(2x - 3y)(2x + 3y)(4x^2 + 9y^2)$

2. Which expression is equivalent to $27x^4 - 6x^2y + 3y^2$?
- Ⓐ $3(3x - y)^2$
- Ⓑ $3(3x^2 + y)^2$
- Ⓒ $3(3x^2 - y)^2$
- Ⓓ $3(3x^2 - y)(3x^2 + y)$

3. Which expression is equivalent to $a^6 - b^6$?
- Ⓐ $(a^2 + b^2)(a^4 - a^2b^2 + b^4)$
- Ⓑ $(a^2 - b^2)(a^4 + a^2b^2 + b^4)$
- Ⓒ $(a + b)^2(a^4 - a^2b^2 + b^4)$
- Ⓓ $(a - b)^2(a^4 + a^2b^2 + b^4)$

4. Which expression is equivalent to $64x^6 - 125y^3$?
- Ⓐ $(4x^2 - 5y)(16x^4 - 20x^2y + 25y^2)$
- Ⓑ $(4x^2 - 5y)(16x^4 + 20x^2y + 25y^2)$
- Ⓒ $(4x^2 - 5y)(4x^2 + 5y)^2$
- Ⓓ $(4x^2 + 5y)(4x^2 - 5y)^2$

5. Which expression is equivalent to $x^3 + 3x^2 - 7x - 21$?
- Ⓐ $(x^2 - 3)(x + 7)$
- Ⓑ $(x^2 + 3)(x - 7)$
- Ⓒ $(x - 3)(x^2 - 7)$
- Ⓓ $(x + 3)(x^2 - 7)$

6. Which expression is equivalent to $4x^3 - 5x^2 - 48x + 60$?
- Ⓐ $(x^2 - 12)(4x - 5)$
- Ⓑ $(x^2 + 12)(4x - 5)$
- Ⓒ $(x^2 - 12)(4x + 5)$
- Ⓓ $(x^2 + 12)(4x + 5)$

7. Which expression is equivalent to $(x-y)^4 - 1$?

   Ⓐ $[(x-y)^2 - 1]^2$

   Ⓑ $[(x-y)^2 - 1][(x+y)^2 + 1]$

   Ⓒ $[(x-y)^2 - 1][(x-y)^2 + 1]$

   Ⓓ $[(x-y)(x+y) - 1][(x-y)(x+y) + 1]$

8. Which is equivalent to the sum of the first 10 terms of the geometric series that begins $24 + 12 + 6 + 3 + \ldots$?

   Ⓐ $\dfrac{24\left(1 - \frac{1}{2^{10}}\right)}{1 - \frac{1}{2}}$

   Ⓑ $\dfrac{24\left(1 - \frac{1}{2^9}\right)}{1 - \frac{1}{2}}$

   Ⓒ $\dfrac{24\left(1 - \frac{1}{2}\right)}{1 - \frac{1}{2^{10}}}$

   Ⓓ $\dfrac{24}{1 - \frac{1}{2}}$

9. Which expression is equivalent to $\frac{49}{9}x^2 - \frac{4}{81}$?

   Ⓐ $\left(\frac{7}{3}x - \frac{2}{9}\right)\left(\frac{7}{3}x + \frac{2}{9}\right)$

   Ⓑ $\left(\frac{7}{3}x - \frac{2}{9}\right)\left(\frac{7}{3}x - \frac{2}{9}\right)$

   Ⓒ $\left(\frac{7}{3}x - \frac{2}{3}\right)\left(\frac{7}{3}x + \frac{2}{3}\right)$

   Ⓓ $\left(\frac{7}{3}x - \frac{2}{3}\right)\left(\frac{7}{3}x - \frac{2}{3}\right)$

10. Which expression is equivalent to $150p^2 - 216$?

    Ⓐ $(5x - 36)(25x + 6)$

    Ⓑ $(30x - 6)(5x + 36)$

    Ⓒ $6(5x - 6)(5x + 6)$

    Ⓓ $6(25x - 36)(25x + 36)$

Name _____

Common Core Standards Practice

HSA.APR.A.1

1. Subtract $(4x^2 + 5y^2 - xy)$ from $(8xy + 3x - y^2 + 2)$.

2. Multiply $(2ab - 3)(a^2 - 3ab + b^2)$.

3. Add $(3p + 5pq - 8 + q)$ and $(2 - 3q + 5p)$.
   - Ⓐ $5pq - 2p + 4q - 10$
   - Ⓑ $5p + 2pq - 3 + q$
   - Ⓒ $5pq + 8p - 2q - 6$
   - Ⓓ $5pq + 8p + 2q + 6$

4. A rectangular prism has a length that is 7 inches longer than its width and a height that is 2 inches shorter than its width.

   Write a polynomial in terms of width w that represents the volume of the prism.

5. The product of two polynomials is $10x^3 - 6x^2 + 20x - 12$. What are the polynomial factors?
   - Ⓐ $(5x^2 + 3)$ and $(2x - 4)$
   - Ⓑ $(5x^2 - 4)$ and $(2x + 3)$
   - Ⓒ $(2x^2 + 4)$ and $(5x - 3)$
   - Ⓓ $(2x^2 - 3)$ and $(5x + 4)$

6. Rae is constructing an open box from a piece of paper that is 6 in. wide and 4.5 in. long. Rae cuts squares of equal size from each corner of the paper, and then folds up the sides of the box.

   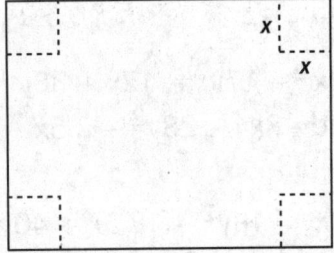

   Write and simplify a polynomial expression for the volume of the box in terms of x.

7. Subtract $(3y^2 + 7y - 20)$ from $(7x^2 + 9y - 18)$.
   - Ⓐ $4x^2 + 2y - 2$
   - Ⓑ $-4x^2 - 2y - 2$
   - Ⓒ $7x^2 - 3y^2 + 2y - 38$
   - Ⓓ $7x^2 - 3y^2 + 2y + 2$

8. Find the product of $(x^2 + x)$ and $(5 - x - 2x^2)$.

9. The sum of two polynomials is $20x^2 - 45y^2 + 18.5x + 37y - 14$. Which polynomials could be the addends? Select all that apply.

   ☐ A. $16x^2 + 12y^2 + 9.5x + 12y - 16$ and $4x^2 - 33y^2 + 9x + 15y + 2$

   ☐ B. $8x^2 - 15y^2 + 10.5x + 20y - 6$ and $12x^2 - 30y^2 + 8x + 17y - 8$

   ☐ C. $-10x^2 + 6y^2 + 12x + 25y + 20$ and $10x^2 - 39y^2 - 6.5x + 12y - 34$

   ☐ D. $12x^2 - 17y^2 + 12x + 38y + 19$ and $-8x^2 - 28y^2 - 2.5x - y - 33$

   ☐ E. $50x^2 - 19y^2 + 18.5x + 40y - 9$ and $-30x^2 - 26y^2 - 3y - 5$

10. Add $8x^3 - 9x^2 + 14x - 24$ and $11x^3 + 14x^2 - 20x - 17$.

11. Subtract $(11c^2d - 12.5c + 15.2d)$ from $(43c^2d + 8.25c + 4.1d + 6.75)$.

    Ⓐ $32c^2d - 4.25c + 20.75d + 6.75$
    Ⓑ $32c^2d + 20.75c - 11.1d + 6.75$
    Ⓒ $54c^2d - 4.25c + 20.75d + 6.75$
    Ⓓ $54c^2d + 20.75c - 11.1d + 6.75$

12. A garden is in the shape of a rectangle. Currently, the width of the garden is 3 meters less than twice the length.

    Write a polynomial that represents the perimeter of the garden if the length, x, is increased by 5 meters and the width is increased by 7 meters.

13. Add $15xy^2 - 6x^2 + 3x - 11y + 30$ and $-8xy^2 + 14x^2 + 5x + 7y - 14$.

    Ⓐ $7xy^2 + 8x^2 + 8x - 4y + 16$
    Ⓑ $-7xy^2 + 8x^2 + 8x - 4y + 16$
    Ⓒ $-23xy^2 - 8x^2 + 2x + 4y - 16$
    Ⓓ $23xy^2 - 8x^2 - 2x + 4y - 16$

14. Subtract $(17a^2 + 4b^2 - 6ab + 80b + 15)$ from $(30a^2 + 9ab - 14b - 1)$.

15. The difference of two polynomials is $19bc^2 + 31b^2 - 12c + 27$. Which polynomials could have been subtracted? Select all that apply.

    ☐ A. $(50bc^2 - 50b^2 - 10c + 30) - (31bc^2 - 81b^2 + 2c + 3)$

    ☐ B. $(17bc^2 + 60b^2 - 8c + 50) - (2bc^2 + 29b^2 - 4c + 23)$

    ☐ C. $(30bc^2 + 20b^2 - 20c + 15) - (11bc^2 - 11b^2 - 8c - 12)$

    ☐ D. $(-66bc^2 + 12b^2 - 16c + 13) - (-85bc^2 - 19b^2 - 4c - 14)$

    ☐ E. $(45bc^2 + 31b^2 - 12c + 27) - (26bc^2 + 31b^2 - 12c + 27)$

16. Add $25x^3 + 32x^2 - 38x + 15$ and $34x^3 - 57x^2 - 38x - 15$.

Name _____

Common Core Standards Practice

HSA.APR.B.2

1. Is $x - 3$ a factor of $P(x) = x^3 - 15x + 18$? If so, write $P(x)$ as a product of two factors.

   Ⓐ yes; $(x - 3)(x^2 - 3x - 6)$
   Ⓑ yes; $(x - 3)(x^2 + 3x - 6)$
   Ⓒ yes; $(x - 3)(x^2 + 3x + 6)$
   Ⓓ no

2. Consider the following equation.
   $-x^3 + 4x^2 - x = -4$

   Part A

   Test several values to find the real-number solution of the equation. Use your solution to wrote a binomial factor of the polynomial $P(x)$ where $P(x) = 0$.

   Part B

   Find the quadratic quotient when you divide the binomial factor in Part A into $P(x)$.

3. Select all the solutions of the equation $x^3 - 2x^2 - x + 2 = 0$.

   ☐ A. $x = 0$
   ☐ B. $x = -1$
   ☐ C. $x = 1$
   ☐ D. $x = -2$
   ☐ E. $x = 2$

4. Given $P(x) = x^3 - 2x^2 - 37x + 14$, if $P(7) = 0$, which of the following is true?

   Ⓐ $x + 7$ is a factor of $x^3 - 2x^2 - 37x + 14$.
   Ⓑ 7 is a factor of $x^3 - 2x^2 - 37x + 14$.
   Ⓒ $x - 7$ is a factor of $x^3 - 2x^2 - 37x + 14$.
   Ⓓ -7 is a factor of $x^3 - 2x^2 - 37x + 14$.

5. Given $P(x) = (x - 4)(x + 5)(x - 8)$, select all of the true statements.

   ☐ A. $P(5) = 0$
   ☐ B. $P(4) = 0$
   ☐ C. $P(8) = 0$
   ☐ D. $P(-4) = 0$
   ☐ E. $P(-05) = 0$

6. Given $P(x) = 5x^3 + 21x^2 + 6x + 8$ what information does $P(0) = 8$ give you?

   Ⓐ x is a factor of polynomial P.
   Ⓑ $x - 8$ is a factor of polynomial P.
   Ⓒ $x + 8$ is a factor of polynomial P.
   Ⓓ x is not a factor of polynomial P.

7. A 3rd degree polynomial has a leading coefficient of 1 and roots $x = -2$, $x = 1$, and $x = 4$. What is the polynomial in expanded form?
   - Ⓐ $x^3 - 3x^2 - 6x + 8$
   - Ⓑ $x^3 + 3x^2 + 6x - 8$
   - Ⓒ $x^3 + 5x^2 + 2x - 8$
   - Ⓓ $x^3 - 5x^2 - 2x + 8$

8. A 3rd degree polynomial has a leading coefficient of 1 and roots $x = -5$, $x = -2$, and $x = 3$. What is the polynomial in expanded form?
   - Ⓐ $x^3 - 4x^2 - 11x + 30$
   - Ⓑ $x^3 + 4x^2 - 11x - 30$
   - Ⓒ $x^3 + 10x^2 + 31x + 30$
   - Ⓓ $x^3 - 10x^2 + 31x - 30$

9. Find all zeros of the equations.

	−5	−3	3	5
$x^3 - 5x^2 - 9x + 45 = 0$	☐	☐	☐	☐
$x^3 - 3x^2 - 25x^2 + 75 = 0$	☐	☐	☐	☐
$x^3 + 5x^2 - 9x - 45 = 0$	☐	☐	☐	☐

10. Select all solutions of the equation $x^3 - 4x^2 - 19x - 14 = 0$.
    - ☐ A. −7
    - ☐ B. 7
    - ☐ C. −2
    - ☐ D. 2
    - ☐ E. −1
    - ☐ F. 1

11. What is the real zero of the polynomial $x^3 + 2x^2 + x + 2$?
    - Ⓐ −2
    - Ⓑ −1
    - Ⓒ 1
    - Ⓓ 2

12. A 2nd degree polynomial $P(x)$ has the following characteristics
    - The leading coefficient is 1.
    - The coefficient of the x-term is 5.
    - $P(6) = 0$

    Use the Remainder Theorem to determine the polynomial. Write your answer in expanded form.

    $P(x) = $

Common Core Standards Practice

HSA.APR.B.3

1. Select all of the steps that could be helpful in graphing function. $f(x) = -4x^2 - 4x + 8$

   ☐ A. Evaluate the function for the vertex, located halfway between the zeros.
   ☐ B. Factor the polynomial expression to find the zeros.
   ☐ C. Substitute $x = 0$ in $f(x)$ to find the y-intercept.
   ☐ D. Draw a straight line through the y-intercept and the vertex.
   ☐ E. Draw a curve through the points.

2. Graph the function $f(x) = -4x^2 - 4x + 8$.

   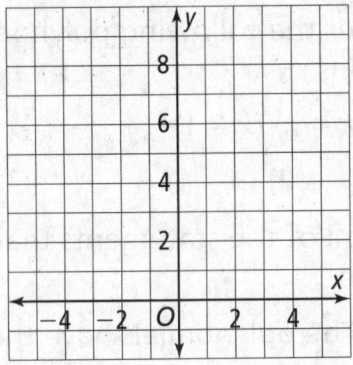

3. Select all the statements that correctly describe the end behavior of the function $f(x) = 3x^3 - 9x^2 - 6x + 18$.

   ☐ A. As $x \to -\infty$, $f(x) \to \infty$.
   ☐ B. As $x \to -\infty$, $f(x) \to -\infty$.
   ☐ C. As $x \to -\infty$, $f(x) \to 0$.
   ☐ D. As $x \to \infty$, $f(x) \to -\infty$.
   ☐ E. As $x \to \infty$, $f(x) \to \infty$.

4. Consider the function $f(x) = (2x + 3)(x^2 - 5x + 6)$.

   Part A

   Select all the zeros of the function.

   ☐ A. 1.5
   ☐ B. 2
   ☐ C. −3
   ☐ D. −1.5
   ☐ E. 3
   ☐ F. −2

   Part B

   What is the y-intercept of the function?

   Ⓐ (0, 9)
   Ⓑ (0, 3)
   Ⓒ (0, −9)
   Ⓓ (0, 18)

   Part C

   Sketch a graph of the function.

   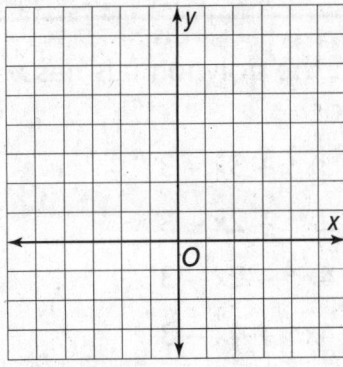

5. What are the zeros and their multiplicities for the function shown in the graph?

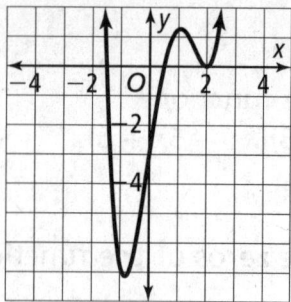

Ⓐ −1.5, 0.5, and 2, each with multiplicity 1

Ⓑ −1.5 and 0.5, each with multiplicity 1, and 2, with multiplicity 2

Ⓒ −0.5 and 1.5, each with multiplicity 2

Ⓓ −3, with multiplicity 4

6. Consider the following polynomial function.

$f(x) = x^3 + x^2 - 20x$

List all three zeros of the function in order.

7. Which of the polynomials has $x - 3$ as a factor?

Ⓐ $x^3 - 3x^2 + 3x - 3$

Ⓑ $x^3 + 2x^2 - 2x + 3$

Ⓒ $x^3 - 4x^2 - 2x - 3$

Ⓓ $x^3 - 4x^2 + 4x - 3$

8. Choose the number of real solutions each equation has.

	0	1	2
$4 - 3x + x^3 = 0$	☐	☐	☐
$-x^2 - 4x + 2 = 0$	☐	☐	☐
$3x^2 - 4x^3 + 1 = 0$	☐	☐	☐

9. Select all the values of x where the function $f(x) = 3x^3 - 2x^2 - x$ is negative.

☐ A. −1
☐ B. −0.25
☐ C. 0.5
☐ D. 1
☐ E. 2

10. Which of the following polynomials has $x + 4$ as a factor?

Ⓐ $x^3 - 2x^2 - 7x - 4$

Ⓑ $x^3 + 4x^2 - x - 4$

Ⓒ $x^3 - 6x^2 + 9x - 4$

Ⓓ $x^3 - 4x^2 - x + 4$

11. Consider the following polynomial functions.

$f(x) = (x + 2)(x - 1)^2$

$g(x) = (x + 2)(x - 1)$

Select all of the statements that are true.

☐ A. The polynomials have the same zeros.

☐ B. The polynomials have the same number of zeros.

☐ C. The end behaviors of the graphs are different.

☐ D. The graphs of $f(x)$ and $g(x)$ are positive over the same intervals.

☐ E. The graphs of $f(x)$ and $g(x)$ cross the x-axis in the same places.

Common Core Standards Practice

HSA.APR.C.4, HSA.APR.C.5

1. Which expression can be rewritten as $(x - 5)(x + 1)$?
   - Ⓐ $(x - 2)^2 + 1$
   - Ⓑ $(x - 2)^2 + 8(x - 2) + 7$
   - Ⓒ $\dfrac{(x + 2)(x^2 - 4x - 5)}{(x - 2)}$
   - Ⓓ $\dfrac{(x - 1)(x^2 - 4x - 5)}{(x - 2)}$

2. $a^3 - 125$ is the product of $(x - 5)$ and which expression?
   - Ⓐ $a^2 + 25$
   - Ⓑ $a^2 - 25$
   - Ⓒ $a^2 + 5a + 25$
   - Ⓓ $a^2 - 5a + 25$

3. $8y^3 + 729$ is the product of $(2y + 9)$ and which expression?
   - Ⓐ $4y^2 + 81$
   - Ⓑ $4y^2 - 81$
   - Ⓒ $4y^2 + 18y + 81$
   - Ⓓ $4y^2 - 18x + 81$

4. Which expressions are equivalent to $(2x - 3)(x + 6)$? Select all that apply.
   - ☐ A. $2x(x + 6) - 3(x + 6)$
   - ☐ B. $x^2 + (-3 + 6)x + (-3)(6)$
   - ☐ C. $x(2x - 3) + 6(2x - 3)$
   - ☐ D. $x(x + 9) + x(x - 18) + 18(x - 1)$
   - ☐ E. $2x^2 + 3x - 18$

5. Given the polynomial identity $(a + b)^5 = (a + b)(a^4 - a^3b + a^2b^2 - ab^3 + b^4)$, which is equivalent to $(4x + 2y)^5$?
   - Ⓐ $(x + y)(256x^4 - 128x^3y - 64x^2y^2 - 32xy^3 + 16)$
   - Ⓑ $(x + y)(256x^4 - 128x^3y + 64x^2y^2 - 32xy^3 + 16)$
   - Ⓒ $(4x + 2y)(256x^4 - 128x^3y - 64x^2y^2 - 32xy^3 + 16)$
   - Ⓓ $(4x + 2y)(256x^4 - 128x^3y + 64x^2y^2 - 32xy^3 + 16)$

6. Which equation is true for all real numbers?
   - Ⓐ $(y + z)^2 = y^2 + z^2$
   - Ⓑ $(y - z)^2 = y^2 - yz + z^2$
   - Ⓒ $(y + z)^3 = y^3 + 3y^2z + 3yz^2 + z^3$
   - Ⓓ $(y - z)^3 = y^3 - 3y^2z - 3yz^2 - z^3$

7. Marissa is working on one side of an equation to trying to prove a polynomial identity. Her work is shown here.

1) $(7x)^2 + (7x^2 - 7)^2 = 49x^2 + (7x^2 - 7)^2$
2) $= 49x^2 + 49x^2 + 49$
3) $= 81x^2 + 49$
4) $= 130x^2$

Which statement about her work is true?

Ⓐ Her work is correct so far.

Ⓑ There is an error in step 2 only.

Ⓒ There is an error in step 4 only.

Ⓓ There are errors in steps 2 and 4.

8. Which expression is equivalent to $(x + y - z)^2$?

Ⓐ $x^2 + y^2 + z^2 - 2xy - 2xz - 2yz$

Ⓑ $x^2 + y^2 + z^2 + 2xy - 2xz - 2yz$

Ⓒ $x^2 + y^2 + z^2 - 2xy - 2xz + 2yz$

Ⓓ $x^2 + y^2 + z^2 - 2xy + 2xz - 2yz$

9. What is the fourth term in the expansion of $(3x + 1)^5$ when written in standard form?

Ⓐ $5x$

Ⓑ $15x$

Ⓒ $15x^2$

Ⓓ $90x^2$

10. Prove algebraically that the difference of the cubes of any two consecutive integers is an odd integer.

Common Core Standards Practice

HSA.APR.D.6, HSA.APR.D.7

1. What is the result of dividing $36x^3 - 15x^2 + 9x$ by $3x$?

   Ⓐ $12x^2$

   Ⓑ $12x^2 - 5x$

   Ⓒ $12x^2 - 5x + 3$

   Ⓓ $12x^3 - 5x^2 + 3x$

2. Which polynomial is the quotient of $(18x^5 - 12x^4 + 20x^3 - 6x^2) \div 2x^2$?

   Ⓐ $9x^3 - 6x^2 + 10x - 3$

   Ⓑ $9x^3 - 6x^2 + 10x - 3x$

   Ⓒ $9x^7 - 6x^6 + 10x^5 - 3x^4$

   Ⓓ $36x^7 - 24x^6 + 40x^5 - 12x^4$

3. Which expression equals $\dfrac{3x^3 - 11x^2 - 22x + 10}{x - 5}$?

   Ⓐ $3x^2 - 2$

   Ⓑ $3x^2 + 4x - 2$

   Ⓒ $3x^2 - 11x - 22 - \dfrac{100}{x - 5}$

   Ⓓ $3x^2 - 11x - 22 + \dfrac{120}{x - 5}$

4. Which expression equals $\dfrac{-2x^3 + 4x^2 + 5x + 7}{x + 3}$?

   Ⓐ $-2x^2 - 5$

   Ⓑ $-2x^2 + 4x - 5$

   Ⓒ $-2x^2 + 10x - 25 - \dfrac{68}{x + 3}$

   Ⓓ $-2x^2 + 10x - 25 + \dfrac{82}{x + 3}$

5. Which expression equals $\dfrac{-2x^3 + 2x^2 + 52x + 48}{x^2 - 2x - 24}$?

   Ⓐ $-2x - 2$

   Ⓑ $-2x + 2$

   Ⓒ $-2x - 2 + \dfrac{96}{x^2 - 2x - 24}$

   Ⓓ $-2x + 2 + \dfrac{96}{x^2 - 2x - 24}$

6. Which expression equals $\dfrac{14x^3 + 6x^2 - 6x + 12}{2x^2 + 5x - 4}$?

   Ⓐ $7x - 13 - \dfrac{6x + 12}{2x^2 + 5x - 4}$

   Ⓑ $7x - 13 + \dfrac{87x - 40}{2x^2 + 5x - 4}$

   Ⓒ $7x + \dfrac{9}{2} - \dfrac{57x + 60}{2(2x^2 + 5x - 4)}$

   Ⓓ $7x + \dfrac{9}{2} - \dfrac{6x + 12}{2x^2 + 5x - 4}$

7. The dimensions of a box for a certain product always have a linear relationship with the variable x. The height of the box is $x - 2$ inches. The volume is $8x^3 + 22x^2 - 31x - 90$. What are the dimensions of the length and width of the box?

8. The volume of a container is $9x^3 - 4x^2 + 3x + 10$ cubic centimeters, and the surface area of the container is $3x^2 - 2x + 7$ square centimeters. Which expression is equal to the ratio of the volume to the surface area of the container?

Ⓐ $3x + 2 - \dfrac{50x + 44}{3x^2 - 2x + 7}$

Ⓑ $3x + \dfrac{2}{3} - \dfrac{50x + 44}{9x^2 - 6x + 21}$

Ⓒ $3x + 2 + \dfrac{16 - 50x}{3x^2 - 2x + 7}$

Ⓓ $3x + \dfrac{2}{3} + \dfrac{16 - 50x}{9x^2 - 6x + 21}$

---

9. Marina says that she can divide any two non-zero polynomial expressions and write the quotient in the form $\dfrac{f(x) + a(x)}{b(x)}$, where $a(x) < b(x)$ and $f(x)$, $a(x)$, and $b(x)$ are all polynomial expressions. Is Marina correct? Choose the best explanation.

Ⓐ She is correct; The quotient of any two non-zero polynomial expressions can be written as $\dfrac{f(x) + a(x)}{b(x)}$.

Ⓑ She is correct; In the remainder of polynomial division $\dfrac{a(x)}{b(x)}$, it must be true that $a(x) < b(x)$.

Ⓒ She is not correct; The quotient of any two non-zero polynomial expressions cannot be written as $\dfrac{f(x) + a(x)}{b(x)}$.

Ⓓ She is not correct; In the remainder of polynomial division $\dfrac{a(x)}{b(x)}$, it must be true that the degree of $a(x)$ is less than the degree of $b(x)$.

10. Let $f(x) = \dfrac{3x + 7}{x^2 - x - 6}$ and $g(x) = \dfrac{2x + 4}{x^2 - 5x + 6}$.

Part A
Find $f(x) + g(x)$.

Part B
Find $f(x) - g(x)$.

Part C
Find $f(x) \cdot g(x)$.

Part D
Find $f(x) \div g(x)$.

Common Core Standards Practice

HSA.CED.A.1

1. A scientist starts an experiment with two types of bacteria. The population of bacteria A after n days is given by the function $F(n) = 3^{n+1}$, and the population of bacteria B after n days is given by the function $G(n) = 27^{2n-1}$.

   Part A

   Select all of the equations that could be used to determine when the population of bacteria A will be the same as the population of bacteria B.

   ☐ A. $3^{n+1} = 27^{2n-1}$
   ☐ B. $3^{n+1} = (3^3)^{2n-1}$
   ☐ C. $n+1 = 3^{2n-1}$
   ☐ D. $3^{n+1} = (3)^{3(2n-1)}$
   ☐ E. $n+1 = 3(2n-1)$

   Part B

   After how many days does the scientist have the same number of both types of bacteria? Write the solution as a decimal.

2. Silvio bought a new car for $16,500. His car loses 15% of its value as soon as he drives it, and then the car will depreciate 18% each year. Which equation can be solved to find the time when the value of Silvio's car is $5,000?

   Ⓐ $5,000 = \$16,500(1 - 0.18)^x$
   Ⓑ $5,000 = \$16,500(1 - 0.15)^x$
   Ⓒ $5,000 = \$14,025(1 - 0.18)^x$
   Ⓓ $5,000 = \$14,025(1 - 0.15)^x$

3. The height of a model rocket, in feet above the ground, can be represented by the function $f(t) = -16t^2 + 300t$, where t is the number of seconds after the rocket is launched.

   Part A

   Write an inequality to represent the times when the rocket is off the ground.

   Part B

   Solve the inequality

   _____

4. The length of a small rectangular garden is four more feet than twice its width, w. The area of the garden must be 30 square feet.

   Part A

   Complete the quadratic equation, in standard form, that models the situation. The right side of the equation should equal 0.

   Part B

   What is the length of the garden, in feet?

5. Consider the triangular piece of fabric shown. What value of x will result in an area of 12 square inches?

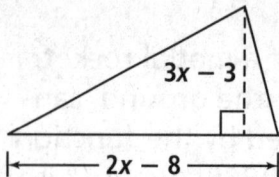

Ⓐ x = 5
Ⓑ x = 6
Ⓒ x = 8
Ⓓ x = 10

6. A flowered area of a park is shaped like a triangle with the dimensions shown. Solve for x. Then find the side lengths of the triangle.

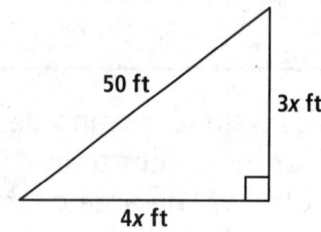

☐ A. 10 ft
☐ B. 20 ft
☐ C. 30 ft
☐ D. 40 ft
☐ E. 60 ft

7. The time t, in seconds, when a rocket is x feet in the air can be modeled by the equation $t(x) = \sqrt{25 - \frac{x}{16}} + 5$. How high in the air is the rocket after 8 seconds?

_____ feet

8. Students are asked to guess the number of marbles in a jar. Any guess that are within 10 of the actual number are considered winning guesses. If there are 245 marbles in the jar, which inequality represents the winning guesses?

Ⓐ $240 \leq x \leq 250$
Ⓑ $235 \leq x \leq 245$
Ⓒ $245 \leq x \leq 255$
Ⓓ $235 \leq x \leq 255$

9. An artist is crafting two cubes out of clay. The smaller cube has side lengths of 4 in. She wants the larger cube to have a volume of 100 in.^{3}. Which equation could she use to find out how much longer the side lengths of the larger cube should be, compared to the side lengths of the smaller cube?

Ⓐ $(100 + x)^3 = 4$
Ⓑ $\sqrt[3]{4 + x} = 100$
Ⓒ $(x + 4)^2 = 100$
Ⓓ $(4 + x)^3 = 100$

10. The volume of a sphere is given by the formula $V = \frac{4}{3}\pi r^3$.

Part A

Write the equation to find the radius of hemisphere with a volume of 90 cm^3.

Part B

What is the radius? Round to the nearest tenth of a centimeter.

Common Core Standards Practice

HSA.CED.A.2

1. Sam has $320 in his bank account at the beginning of the year. Every two weeks he deposits his $150 paycheck. Every week he withdraws $40 for expenses.

   Part A
   Which equations model how much money M is in Sam's account for week w? Select all that apply.

   ☐ A. $M = 320 + \frac{1}{2}(150)w - 40w$
   ☐ B. $M = 320 + 35w$
   ☐ C. $M = 320 + 2(150)w - 40w$
   ☐ D. $M = 320 - 2(150)w + 40w$
   ☐ E. $M = 320 - \frac{1}{2}(150)w + 40w$

   Part B
   How much money, in dollars, will be in the account after 10 weeks?

2. Thao rides a bicycle to and from the post office. Her average speed is the same both ways. Thao's distance from home d, in kilometers, x minutes after she starts, is modeled by the function $d(x) = 5 - \frac{1}{4}|x - 20|$.

   How far will Thao be from home 24 minutes after she starts her bike ride? Write your answer in miles.

3. A machine produces metal rods. The length f of the rods, in centimeters, as a function of the diameter, x, is modeled by $f(x) = 17 - |2x - 3|$.

   Part A
   Graph the function.

   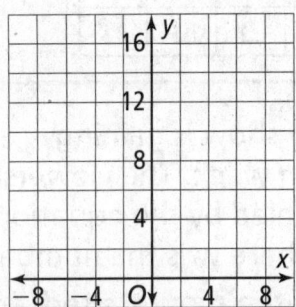

   Part B
   If the diameter of the rod is 5 cm what is the length, in cm?

4. Amelia buys a new car for $18,000. She believes it will lose about 12% of its value per year.

   Part A
   What equation could she graph to determine when the car will be worth $8,000 or less?

   Ⓐ $V = 18,000(-0.12)t$
   Ⓑ $V = 18,000(1.12)t$
   Ⓒ $V = 18,000(1 - 0.12)t$
   Ⓓ $V = 18,000(0.88)t$

   Part B
   By what year will Amelia's car be worth $8,000 or less? Write your answer as a whole number.

5. The number of people visiting a museum throughout the day can be modeled by the equation $y = -7.5x^2 + 60x$, where x is the number of hours after the museum opens. Determine the number of people visiting the museum at different times of the day.

	0	60	90	120
2 hours	☐	☐	☐	☐
4 hours	☐	☐	☐	☐
6 hours	☐	☐	☐	☐
8 hours	☐	☐	☐	☐

6. A streaming show is gaining viewers each week. The viewership can be modeled by the equation $V = \frac{1}{22}w^3$ where w is the number of weeks since the show started, and V is thousands of viewers. Select the two sets of steps that you could use to predict when viewership would reach 100,000.

   ☐ A. Solve the equation $100{,}000 = \frac{1}{22}x^3$.

   ☐ B. Graph $V = \frac{1}{22}x^3$ and find the w-value that corresponds to $V = 100$.

   ☐ C. Graph $V = \frac{1}{22}x^3$ and find the w-value that corresponds to $V = 100{,}000$.

   ☐ D. Graph $V = \frac{1}{22}x^3$ and the horizontal line $V = 100{,}000$ on the same coordinate plane. Find the w-value of the point where they intersect.

   ☐ E. Graph $V = \frac{1}{22}x^3$ and the horizontal line $V = 100$ on the same coordinate plane. Find the w-value of the point where they intersect.

7. The equation $y = -16x^2 + 32x$ represents the height of ball x seconds after being kicked. Use a graph to determine the time when the ball is kicked and when it hits the ground.

   ☐ A. 0 s   ☐ D. 16 s
   ☐ B. 1 s   ☐ E. 32 s
   ☐ C. 2 s

8. The graph shows the amount of money that Andre has saved after x month. Use the graph to predict how much money Andre will have saved after 8 months.

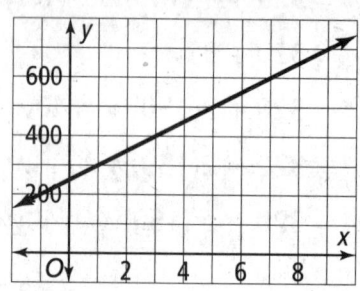

   Ⓐ $400   Ⓒ $650
   Ⓑ $600   Ⓓ $700

9. The function $d(h) = 1.22\sqrt{h}$ gives the approximate distance to the horizon d, for height above sea level in feet, h. Use the graph to predict the distance to the horizon of a viewer 16 feet above sea level. Round your answer to the nearest mile.

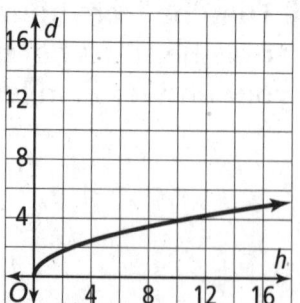

enVision® Algebra 2   Common Core Standards Practice Workbook

Common Core Standards Practice

HSA.CED.A.3

1. The total price of two sweatshirts is $95. The difference in their prices is $7. Which equations and inequalities represent this situation? Select all that apply.

   ☐ A. $x < 0$ ☐ E. $x + y = 95$
   ☐ B. $y < 0$ ☐ F. $x - y = 7$
   ☐ C. $x > 0$ ☐ G. $2x = 95$
   ☐ D. $y > 0$ ☐ H. $x - 7 = y$

2. An ice cream shop sold 215 cones of ice cream on a Saturday. They sell small cones of ice cream for $5 and large cones for $7. If they earned at least $1,200 selling ice cream cones, is it possible that they sold 160 small cones? Explain.

3. Tickets to a concert sold for $18 if purchased in advance. Any tickets sold on the day of the show sold for $22. The concert hall sold 475 tickets for a total of $9,450. Let x represent the number of advance tickets sold and y represent the number of tickets sold on the day of the show. Write a system of equations to represent this situation.

4. A souvenir shop sells t-shirts for $20 and baseball hats for $25. They earned less than $950 from sales one day. Is it possible that they sold 29 t-shirts and 13 baseball hats? Explain.

5. Which restrictions are represented in the shaded area of the graph?

   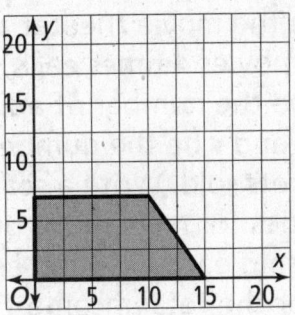

   Ⓐ $7 \geq y \geq 0$
      $x \geq 0$
      $7x + 5y \geq 105$

   Ⓑ $7 \geq y \geq 0$
      $x \geq 0$
      $7x + 5y \leq 105$

   Ⓒ $7 \geq x \geq 0$
      $y \geq 0$
      $7x + 5y \geq 105$

   Ⓓ $7 \geq x \geq 0$
      $y \geq 0$
      $7x + 5y < 105$

6. Carli has a collection of 50 nickels and dimes. She has at least 10 of each coin. Her collection is worth at least $3.00. Let n be the number of nickels and d be the number of dimes in her collection. Which set of equations and inequalities models the situation?

Ⓐ $10 \leq n + d \leq 50$; $5n + 10d \leq 300$

Ⓑ $10 \leq n + d \leq 50$; $5n + 10d \geq 300$

Ⓒ $n \geq 10$; $d \geq 10$; $n + d = 50$; $5n + 10d \geq 300$

Ⓓ $n \geq 10$; $d \geq 10$; $n + d = 50$; $5n + 10d \leq 300$

---

7. A movie theater sells tickets for $13 for adults and $11 for children under the age of 12. There are 275 seats in the movie theater and they show movies 4 times each day. Let a be the number of adult tickets sold and c be the number of child tickets sold. Write a set of inequalities for restrictions on the tickets sold each day, and an equation for the total income T from tickets sold.

---

8. A used book store wants to buy no more than 300 books to fill a new bookshelf in the store. Write a set of restrictions based on the information in the table and an equation for the profit P. Let x represent the number of paperback books and y represent the number of hardcover books.

	Paperback	Hardcover
Cost	$1.50	$3.00
Selling Price	$6.00	$12.00

---

9. Karina earns $12 per hour babysitting for b hours. She also earns $15 per hour at the grocery store for g hours. Karina will do both jobs, but work no more than 20 hours each week. She wants to earn at least $180 each week. Which set of inequalities models this situation?

Ⓐ $12b + 15g \leq 180$
   $b \geq 0$; $g \geq 0$
   $b + d \leq 20$

Ⓑ $12b + 15g \leq 180$
   $b \geq 0$; $g \geq 0$
   $b + d \geq 20$

Ⓒ $12b + 15g \geq 180$
   $b > 0$; $g > 0$
   $b + d \leq 20$

Ⓓ $12b + 15g \geq 180$
   $b > 0$; $g > 0$
   $b + d \geq 20$

Name _____

Common Core Standards Practice

HSA.CED.A.4

1. The volume of a rectangular prism can be found using the formula $V = lwh$, where l is the length, w is the width, and h is the height of the prism. Solve the formula for h.

   Ⓐ $h = V/lw$
   Ⓑ $h = \frac{lw}{V}$
   Ⓒ $h = \frac{Vl}{w}$
   Ⓓ $h = \frac{V}{lw}$

2. The area of a circle can be calculated using the formula $A = \pi r^2$, where r is the radius of the circle. Solve the formula for r.

3. The area of a triangle can be found using the formula $A = \frac{1}{2}bh$, where b is the length of the base of the triangle, and h is the height of the triangle. Solve the formula for h.

4. The volume of a cylinder can be found using the formula $V = \pi r^2 h$, where r is the radius of the base of the cylinder and h is the height of the cylinder. Which of the following equations are the volume formula correctly solved for another variable? Select all true equations.

   ☐ A. $h = \frac{V}{\pi r^2}$
   ☐ B. $h = \sqrt{\frac{V}{\pi r^2}}$
   ☐ C. $r = \frac{V}{\pi h}$
   ☐ D. $r = \sqrt{\frac{V}{\pi h}}$
   ☐ E. $r = \frac{V}{\pi h^2}$

5. The formula $F = \frac{9}{5}C + 32$ can be used to convert temperatures in degrees Celsius to degrees Fahrenheit. Solve the formula for C.

   Ⓐ $C = \frac{5}{9}F - 32$
   Ⓑ $C = \frac{5}{9}(F - 32)$
   Ⓒ $C = \frac{5}{9F - 32}$
   Ⓓ $C = \frac{5}{9(F - 32)}$

6. The volume of a cone can be found using the formula $V = \frac{1}{3}\pi r^2 h$, where r is the radius of the base of the cone and h is the height of the cone. Solve the formula for r.

   Ⓐ $r = \sqrt{\frac{3V}{\pi h}}$

   Ⓑ $r = \frac{3V}{\pi h}$

   Ⓒ $r^2 = \frac{3V}{\pi h}$

   Ⓓ $r = \sqrt{\frac{V}{3\pi h}}$

7. The volume of a sphere can be found using the formula $V = \frac{4}{3}\pi r^3$, where r is the radius of the sphere. Solve the formula for r.

   Ⓐ $r = \sqrt[3]{\frac{4V}{3\pi}}$

   Ⓑ $r^3 = \frac{3V}{4\pi}$

   Ⓒ $r = \sqrt[3]{\frac{3V}{4\pi}}$

   Ⓓ $r = \sqrt{\frac{3V}{4\pi}}$

8. The area of a square can be found using the formula $A = s^2$, where s is the length of a side of the square. Solve the formula for s.

9. The volume of a pyramid with a rectangular base can be found using the formula $V = \frac{1}{3}lwh$, where l is the length of the base, w is the width of the base, and h is the height of the pyramid. Which of the following equations are the volume formula correctly solved for another variable? Select all true equations.

   ☐ A. $h = \frac{V}{3lw}$

   ☐ B. $h = \frac{3V}{lw}$

   ☐ C. $w = \frac{V}{3lh}$

   ☐ D. $l = \frac{3V}{wh}$

   ☐ E. $w = \frac{3V}{lh}$

10. The Pythagorean Theorem relates the lengths a and b of the legs of a right triangle to the length c of the hypotenuse with the formula $a^2 + b^2 = c^2$. Which of the following equations is the Pythagorean Theorem solved for b?

    Ⓐ $b^2 = c^2 - a^2$

    Ⓑ $b = \sqrt{c^2 - a^2}$

    Ⓒ $b = \sqrt{a^2 - c^2}$

    Ⓓ $b = c^2 - a^2$

Common Core Standards Practice

HSA.REI.A.2

1. Solve the equation $\sqrt{3x-1} = 3x - 7$. Identify the extraneous solution. Write your answers as reduced fractions, if necessary.

   Solution: $x =$

   Extraneous solution: $x =$

2. Solve the radical equation $\sqrt{x+1} = \sqrt{x} + 1$.

   Ⓐ $x = -1$
   Ⓑ $x = 0$
   Ⓒ $x = 1$
   Ⓓ $x = 3$

3. Which equation has an extraneous solution at $x = 0$?

   Ⓐ $x + 4 = \sqrt{x + 10}$
   Ⓑ $\sqrt{x+4} = x - 2$
   Ⓒ $\sqrt{x+2} = x - 4$
   Ⓓ $\sqrt{x} = x - 6$

4. Solve the equation $5(x^2 + x + 2)^{\frac{1}{2}} = 10$. Do not select any extraneous solutions.

   ☐ A. $x = -2$
   ☐ B. $x = -1$
   ☐ C. $x = 0$
   ☐ D. $x = 1$
   ☐ E. $x = 2$

5. Solve the radical equation $\sqrt{x+9} = x - 3$. Check for extraneous solutions.

	0	3	7
Solution(s)	☐	☐	☐
Extraneous Solution(s)	☐	☐	☐

6. Solve the radical equation $\sqrt{x} - \sqrt{49 - x} = 7$. Identify the extraneous solution. Write your answers as reduced fractions, if necessary.

   Solution: $x =$

   Extraneous solution: $x =$

7. Solve the equation $(x^2 + x + 1)^{\frac{1}{3}} = 1$. Do not select any extraneous solutions.

   ☐ A. $x = -2$
   ☐ B. $x = -1$
   ☐ C. $x = 0$
   ☐ D. $x = 1$
   ☐ E. $x = 2$

8. Which equation has an extraneous solution at $x = 1$?

   Ⓐ $\sqrt{x + 15} = x + 3$
   Ⓑ $\sqrt{x + 35} = 7 - x$
   Ⓒ $\sqrt{17 - x} = x - 5$
   Ⓓ $\sqrt{1 - x} = x - 1$

9. Solve the radical equation $\sqrt{x + 25} = x - 5$. Check for extraneous solutions.

   Ⓐ $x = 0$ or $x = 11$
   Ⓑ $x = 0$
   Ⓒ $x = 11$
   Ⓓ no solution

10. Solve the radical equation $\sqrt{x + 8} = 12 - x$. Write your answers as reduced fractions, if necessary.

    Solution: $x =$

    Extraneous solution: $x =$

11. Solve the radical equation $\sqrt{x + 3} = x - 3$. Write your answers as reduced fractions, if necessary.

    Solution: $x =$

    or $x =$

12. Solve the equation $\sqrt{3x - 6} = x - 2$. Check for extraneous solutions. Select all solutions.

    ☐ A. -2
    ☐ B. 2
    ☐ C. -5
    ☐ D. 5
    ☐ E. $\frac{1}{2}$

13. Solve the radical equation $\sqrt{x + 5} = 15 - x$. Check for extraneous solutions.

    Ⓐ $x = 11$ or $x = 20$
    Ⓑ $x = 11$
    Ⓒ $x = 20$
    Ⓓ no solution

14. Which equation has an extraneous solution at $x = -3$?

    Ⓐ $\sqrt{x + 19} = 1 - x$
    Ⓑ $\sqrt{6 - x} = -x$
    Ⓒ $\sqrt{x + 7} = x + 5$
    Ⓓ $\sqrt{x + 7} = x + 1$

Common Core Standards Practice

HSA.REI.D.11

1. At what x-values do the graphs of $f(x) = 2x^3 + 2$ and $g(x) = 3(x - 1) + 5$ intersect? Select all that apply.
   - ☐ A. $-\frac{49}{40}$
   - ☐ B. $-\frac{5}{4}$
   - ☐ C. 0
   - ☐ D. $\frac{5}{4}$
   - ☐ E. $\frac{49}{40}$

2. How many points of intersection are there between the graphs of $y = 9 - 4x$ and $y = \frac{3}{(x+1)}$?
   - Ⓐ 0
   - Ⓑ 1
   - Ⓒ 2
   - Ⓓ 3

3. Find the solutions of the system of equations: $f(x) = 5(x - 1)^2 - 8$ and $g(x) = |5x - 6|$. Round coordinates to the nearest thousandth if necessary.

4. Find the solutions of the system of equations: $f(x) = 1.56^x - 3$ and $y = 2x - 3$. Round coordinates to the nearest thousandth if necessary.

5. This table shows function values of continuous functions $f(x)$ and $g(x)$ rounded to the nearest thousandth.

x	f(x)	g(x)
−10	5	−78
−6	−4.999	18
−2	−4.889	−30
2	4	−30
6	724	210
10	59,044	882

   In which intervals do $f(x)$ and $g(x)$ intersect? Select all that apply.
   - ☐ A. $-10 < x < -6$
   - ☐ B. $-6 < x < -2$
   - ☐ C. $-2 < x < 2$
   - ☐ D. $2 < x < 6$
   - ☐ E. $6 < x < 10$

6. Which are the solutions to the equation $5 \ln(x^2 + 1) = -\frac{1}{2}x + 7$? Coordinates are rounded to the nearest thousandth. Select all that apply.
   - ☐ A. (−1.987, 7.993)
   - ☐ B. (−1.570, 6.215)
   - ☐ C. (1.570, 6.215)
   - ☐ D. (1.987, 7.993)
   - ☐ E. (8.298, 11.149)
   - ☐ F. (9.736, 11.868

7. The population of Arlington in 2020 was 8,532 and was growing at an annual rate of 0.8%. The nearby town of Greenville had a population of 7,648 and was growing at an annual rate of 1.2%. If these patterns continue, in what year will the population of Greenville first be greater the population of Arlington? Explain.

8. The paths of two birds are plotted on a coordinate plane and their equations are represented by $y = 1.25^x + 1$ and $y = \dfrac{5}{(x+1)}$ from $0 < x < 5$. What is the intersection point of their flight paths? Round coordinates to the nearest thousandth if necessary.

9. Complete the table to show how many points of intersection the graph of $f(x) = 0.2x - 5$ has with each function.

Function	Number of intersections
$g(x) = \dfrac{x}{x-4}$	
$h(x) = -2\|x^2 - 3x + 6\|$	
$j(x) = \log(x - 3)$	
$k(x) = (x-2)^2(x+3)^2$	

10. Graph the functions $f(x) = x^3 - x^2 - 5x - 1$ and $g(x) = \dfrac{(3+x)}{2(x-3)}$. How many solutions are there to the system of $f(x)$ and $g(x)$? Where do the graphs intersect? Round answers to the nearest thousandth if necessary.

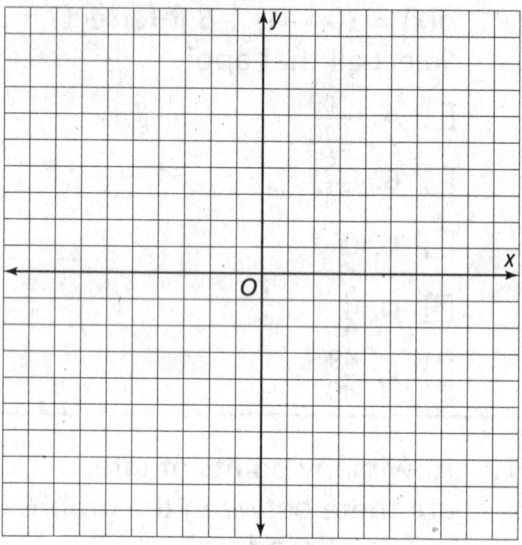

Common Core Standards Practice

HSF.IF.B.4, HSF.IF.B.5

1. While flying above the water, a bird dives toward a fish and then returns to its original height. The function $f(x) = 4x^2 - 4$ represents the path of the bird's dive, where x is the horizontal distance from the fish, and $f(x)$ is its height above the water. Select all statements about the function that make sense in context.

   ☐ A. The domain is all real numbers.

   ☐ B. The range is $[-4, y]$, where y is its original height.

   ☐ C. The minimum is the point where the bird touches the surface of the water.

   ☐ D. The y-intercept is the depth of the fish.

   ☐ E. The function is negative wherever the bird is diving.

   ☐ F. The function is symmetric.

2. An employee takes a cup of soup to work, but forgets about it and it stays in the fridge for the rest of the year. What property of the function representing the temperature of the soup over time indicates that it will continue cooling, but never freeze?

   Ⓐ The y-intercept of the function is room temperature.

   Ⓑ The function decreases to a maximum, then increases.

   Ⓒ There is a horizontal asymptote of the function.

   Ⓓ The end behavior of the function is that as $x \to \infty$, $f(x) \to \infty$.

3. The graph of the function $f(x) = x^2 + 7x$ represents the shape of a canyon at the foot of a mountain. What point most likely represents the lowest point in the canyon?

   Ⓐ $(-3.5, -12.25)$

   Ⓑ $(0, 7)$

   Ⓒ $(-7, 0)$

   Ⓓ $(3.5, -12.25)$

The table, with values in inches, represents the path of a basketball as it is dribbled before being picked up for a shot. Use the table for Items 4–5.

x	−6	−5	■	−3	−2	−1	0
y	7	1	■	1	7	17	31

4. A game developer uses the parabola passing through the points in the table to model animations in a game. What is the vertex?

5. Why might the vertex of the parabola not make sense in context?

   Ⓐ The point isn't listed in the table.

   Ⓑ The point has a negative x-value.

   Ⓒ The point has a negative y-value.

   Ⓓ The path of the ball does not have a minimum point.

The length of time f(x), in seconds, that it takes a pendulum of length x meters to swing from one side to the other and back is approximated by a square root function. Use the function for Items 6–7.

6. A pendulum of length 4 meters has a period of about 4 seconds, and a pendulum of length 9 meters has a period of about 6 seconds. Sketch a graph the function.

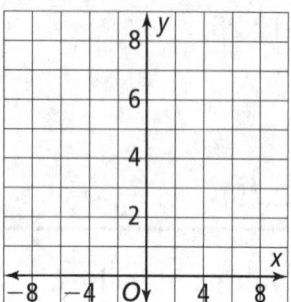

7. Suppose pendulum A has a period of 20 seconds and pendulum B has a period of 15 seconds. Is pendulum B longer or shorter than pendulum A, and why?

   Ⓐ Longer, because the function is positive on its domain.

   Ⓑ Shorter, because the function is positive on its domain.

   Ⓒ Longer, because the function is increasing on its domain.

   Ⓓ Shorter, because the function is increasing on its domain.

8. The volume of helium in a balloon is modeled by the function $y = -1.1x^3 + 3x^2 + 1$, where x is the number of seconds after the helium tank is turned on. What point on the graph represents the volume of helium in the balloon just before the tank was turned on?

9. An elevator takes 32 seconds to descend from floor 2 of a building to sub-basement 2 at a constant rate, then rises for 24 seconds at a different speed, passing the lobby after only 8 seconds. Sketch a graph of the function representing the height of the elevator during this time if the lobby is floor 0 and the elevator reaches its minimum height at time 0.

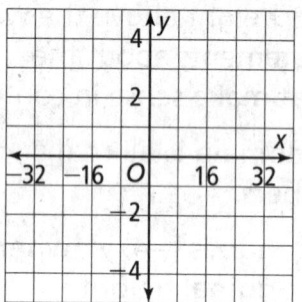

10. Corin graphed the function h(t) that shows the height, in feet, of a ball and the time, in seconds, after she threw into the air. What is a reasonable domain for h(t)?

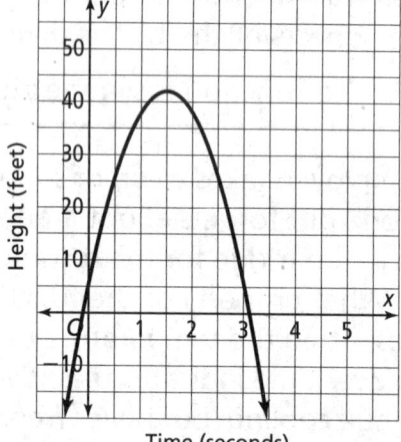

   Ⓐ positive real numbers less than or equal to 42

   Ⓑ whole numbers less than or equal to 42

   Ⓒ positive real numbers less than or equal to 3.1

   Ⓓ whole numbers less than or equal to 3

Common Core Standards Practice

HSF.IF.B.6

1. The graph of a function f is shown. Use the graph to estimate the average rate of change from $x = -2$ to $x = 2$.

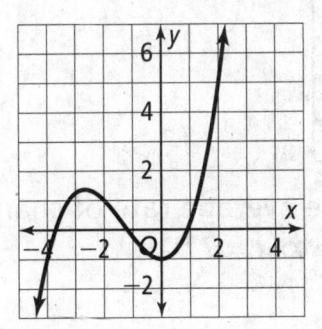

   Ⓐ 1
   Ⓑ 2
   Ⓒ 4
   Ⓓ 5

2. Consider the function $f(x) = \sqrt{x+1}$. What is the average rate of change from $x = 0$ to $x = 3$?

   Ⓐ $\frac{1}{3}$ Ⓒ 1
   Ⓑ $\frac{2}{3}$ Ⓓ 3

3. Consider the function in the table.

x	f(x)
-2	8
-1	5
0	4
1	5
2	8

   What is the average rate of change from $x = -2$ to $x = 2$? Express your answer as a reduced fraction, if necessary.

4. Over which intervals is the average rate of change of $f(x) = x^2 + 7x + 4$ positive. Select all that apply.

   ☐ A. $x = -7$ to $x = -1$
   ☐ B. $x = -5$ to $x = 0$
   ☐ C. $x = -5$ to $x = -2$
   ☐ D. $x = -4$ to $x = -2$
   ☐ E. $x = -2$ to $x = 0$

5. The graph of the function f is shown. Use the graph to estimate the average rate of change from $x = -1$ to $x = 2$.

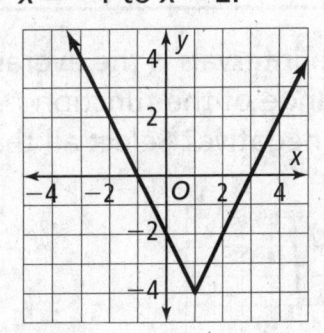

   Ⓐ -2
   Ⓑ $-\frac{2}{3}$
   Ⓒ $\frac{2}{3}$
   Ⓓ 2

6. Determine the average rate of change of the function $f(x) = -|x + 5|$ over each of the intervals.

	$-\frac{2}{3}$	0	1
$x = -8$ to $x = -2$	☐	☐	☐
$x = -6$ to $x = 0$	☐	☐	☐
$x = -9$ to $x = -6$	☐	☐	☐

7. Consider the function $f(x) = 2^{x-2}$. What is the average rate of change from $x = 0$ to $x = 4$?

8. The graph of the function f is shown. Use the graph to estimate the average rate of change from $x = 1$ to $x = 6$.

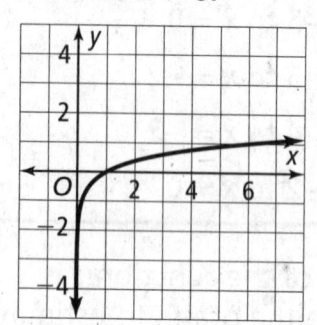

9. Over which intervals is the average rate of change of the function f in the graph negative? Select all that apply.

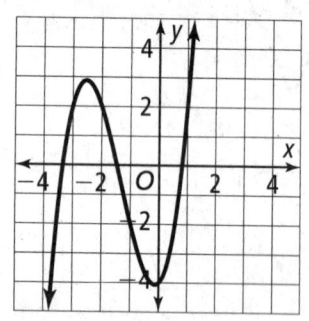

- [ ] A. $x = -3$ to $x = 0$
- [ ] B. $x = -2$ to $x = -1$
- [ ] C. $x = -1$ to $x = 1$
- [ ] D. $x = -3$ to $x = 1$
- [ ] E. $x = -2$ to $x = 2$

10. Consider the function $f(x) = 2^{x-2}$. What is the average rate of change from $x = 2$ to $x = 6$?

11. Consider the function in the table.

x	f(x)
-2	0
-1	1
2	2
7	3

What is the average rate of change from $x = 2$ to $x = 7$?

Ⓐ -5
Ⓑ $-\frac{1}{5}$
Ⓒ $\frac{1}{5}$
Ⓓ 5

12. Consider the function $f(x) = x^3 - 4x^2 - 5x$. What is the average rate of change from $x = -1$ to $x = 4$?

Ⓐ -20
Ⓑ -5
Ⓒ -4
Ⓓ 4

Common Core Standards Practice

HSF.IF.C.7

1. Select the three statements that together define the piecewise function f, shown in the graph.

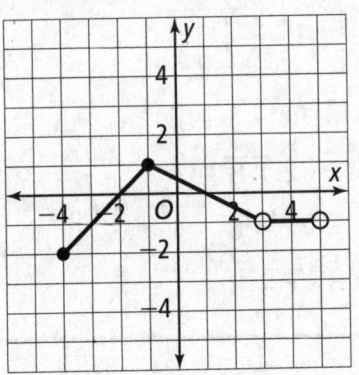

   ☐ A. $f(x) = x + 2, -4 \leq x < -1$
   ☐ B. $f(x) = x + 2, -4 < x < -1$
   ☐ C. $f(x) = -\left(\frac{1}{2}\right)(x - 1), -1 \leq x \leq 3$
   ☐ D. $f(x) = -\left(\frac{1}{2}\right)(x - 1), -1 \leq x < 3$
   ☐ E. $f(x) = -1, 3 < x < 5$
   ☐ F. $f(x) = -1, 3 \leq x \leq 5$

2. An equation that represents the path of a diver jumping off a diving board is $y = -6x^2 + 4x + 3.5$, where y is the height and x is the horizontal distance from the board, in meters. Graph this function from the point where the diver jumped to the point where they reach the water.

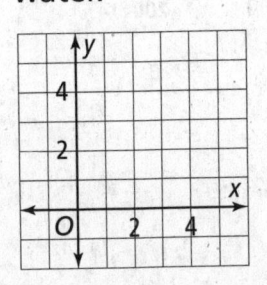

3. Which of the following absolute value functions defines the function shown in the graph?

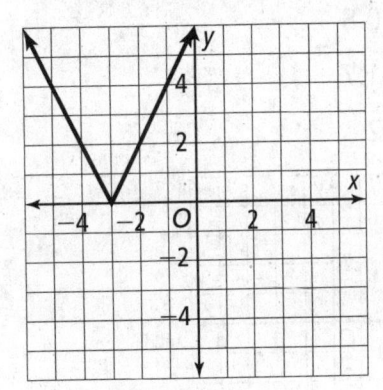

   Ⓐ $f(x) = |2x - 6|$
   Ⓑ $f(x) = 2|x - 3|$
   Ⓒ $f(x) = |2x + 3|$
   Ⓓ $f(x) = 2|x + 3|$

4. What radical function is represented by the graph?

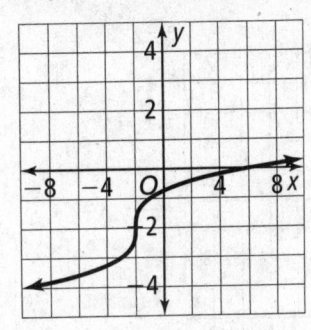

   Ⓐ $f(x) = \sqrt[3]{x + 2} - 2$
   Ⓑ $f(x) = \sqrt[3]{x - 2} + 2$
   Ⓒ $f(x) = \sqrt[3]{x - 1} + 1$
   Ⓓ $f(x) = \sqrt[3]{x + 1} - 1$

5. Sketch a graph of the function $f(x) = 2x^3 - 5x^2 + 2$ and select the approximate f-values of all relative maxima and minima of the function.

☐ A. −2.6
☐ B. −0.6
☐ C. 0.8
☐ D. 1.7
☐ E. 2

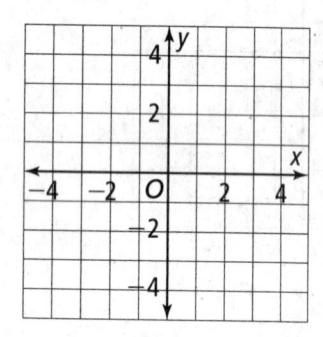

6. Graph $f(x) = \sqrt{x} + 4$. Write the domain and range of the function as inequalities with the variables on the left.

Domain:

Range:

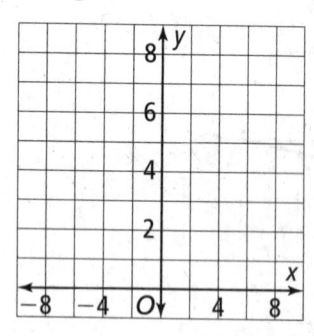

7. What radical function is represented by the graph?

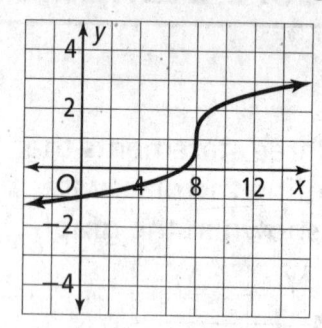

Ⓐ $f(x) = \sqrt[3]{x-1} + 2$
Ⓑ $f(x) = \sqrt{x+8} - 1$
Ⓒ $f(x) = \sqrt[3]{x-8} + 1$
Ⓓ $f(x) = \sqrt[3]{x+8} - 1$

8. The seagull population of Gainesville was 154,000 in 2017. It is expected to decrease by about 5.3% per year. The exponential decay function of the seagull population, $P(t)$, t years after 2017. is given by the equation. Graph the function.

$P(t) = 154{,}000(0.947)^t$

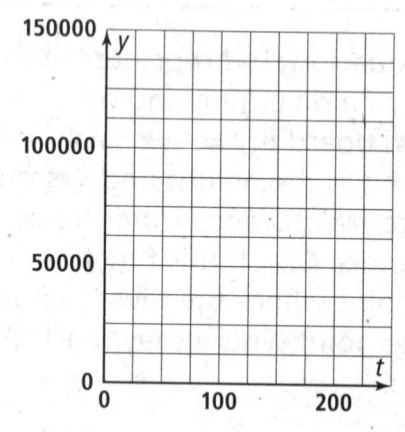

Common Core Standards Practice

HSF.IF.C.8

1. Sarah invests $1,500 in an account that earns 5.2% interest, compounded quarterly. The amount after t years can be modeled by the function $A(t) = 1500(1.013)^{4t}$. What is the effective annual interest rate of $A(t)$, rounded to the nearest thousandth of a percent?

2. For a quadratic function, identify the form that shows the positive or negative value(s) of each given property.

	standard	factored	vertex
maximum	☐	☐	☐
x-intercept(s)	☐	☐	☐
y-intercept	☐	☐	☐
zeros	☐	☐	☐
range	☐	☐	☐
axis of symmetry	☐	☐	☐

3. The height of a ball t seconds after being kicked can be modeled by the function $h(t) = -16t^2 + vt$, where v is the initial upward velocity of the kick in feet per second. If the ball lands after 2.5 seconds, what is the initial upward velocity of the ball, in feet per second? Round to the nearest tenth, if necessary.

4. Select all expressions that are factors of the quadratic function $f(x) = 2x^2 + 4x - 16$.
   - ☐ A. $x + 4$
   - ☐ B. $x - 4$
   - ☐ C. $x\sqrt{2} + 4$
   - ☐ D. $x\sqrt{2} - 4$
   - ☐ E. $2x - 4$

5. Which function is the quadratic function $f(x) = x^2 + 10x + 24$ written in vertex form?
   - Ⓐ $f(x) = (x + 10)^2 + 24$
   - Ⓑ $f(x) = (x + 5)^2 + 24$
   - Ⓒ $f(x) = (x + 5)^2 - 1$
   - Ⓓ $f(x) = (x + 5)^2 + 1$

6. Which function is the quadratic function $f(x) = x^2 - 13x + 42$ written in factored form?
   - Ⓐ $f(x) = (x + 14)(x + 3)$
   - Ⓑ $f(x) = (x - 14)(x - 3)$
   - Ⓒ $f(x) = (x + 6)(x + 7)$
   - Ⓓ $f(x) = (x - 6)(x - 7)$

7. Select all functions that are equivalent to $f(x) = -x^2 + 6x + 16$.
   - ☐ A. $f(x) = -(x - 3)^2 + 16$
   - ☐ B. $f(x) = (x - 3)^2 - 25$
   - ☐ C. $f(x) = -(x - 8)(x + 2)$
   - ☐ D. $f(x) = -(x + 8)(x - 2)$
   - ☐ E. $f(x) = -(x - 3)^2 + 25$

8. Select all true statements about the quadratic function $f(x) = a(x - h)^2 + k$.

   ☐ A. If $a > 0$, then the domain is $[h, \infty)$.

   ☐ B. If $a > 0$, then the range is $[h, \infty)$.

   ☐ C. If h is a zero of $f(x)$, then $k = 0$.

   ☐ D. If $(x - b)$ is a factor, then one of the zeros is b.

   ☐ E. If $(x - b)$ is a factor, then one of the zeros is $\frac{-b}{2a}$.

9. Jillian opened an account with an initial investment of $4,500. The account earns 2.5% annual interest. The amount in her account t years from today can be modeled by the function $A(t) = 4500(1.025)^{t+4}$. What does the +4 in the exponent represent?

   Ⓐ The interest is compounded quarterly.

   Ⓑ Jillian invested another $4,500 four times.

   Ⓒ Jillian will withdraw the money from her account in 4 years.

   Ⓓ Jillian opened the account 4 years ago.

10. The function f is written in three ways:

    $f(x) = 2x^2 - 10x - 12$

    $f(x) = 2(x - 6)(x + 1)$

    $f(x) = 2\left(x - \frac{5}{2}\right)^2 - \frac{49}{2}$

    What is the axis of symmetry of the graph of f?

    Ⓐ $x = 5$ 　　Ⓒ $x = \frac{5}{2}$

    Ⓑ $x = 10$ 　　Ⓓ $x = \frac{7}{2}$

11. Is the vertex of the quadratic function $f(x) = 4x^2 - 40x - 104$ a minimum or maximum point? Explain.

    Ⓐ maximum, because the leading coefficient 4 is positive.

    Ⓑ minimum, because the leading coefficient 4 is positive.

    Ⓒ maximum, because the ratio $\frac{40}{2(4)}$ is positive.

    Ⓢ minimum, because the ratio $\frac{-40}{2(4)}$ is negative.

12. Mike is studying a bacterial culture that is estimated to have a growth factor of approximately 1.09 per day. If he starts with a culture of 0.5 cm^2 and checks on it once a week, what function describes how large he should expect it to be after w weeks?

    Ⓐ $S(w) = 0.5(1.09)^{\frac{1}{7}w}$

    Ⓑ $S(w) = 0.5(1.09)^{7w}$

    Ⓒ $S(w) = 0.5(1.09^7)^{\frac{1}{7}w}$

    Ⓓ $S(w) = 0.5\left(1.09^{\frac{1}{7}}\right)^{7w}$

Common Core Standards Practice

HSF.IF.C.9

1. The volume of a cube with edge lengths x is $V(x) = x^3$. The volume of a sphere with diameter x is shown in the graph. When $x = 1.5$, which volume is greater?

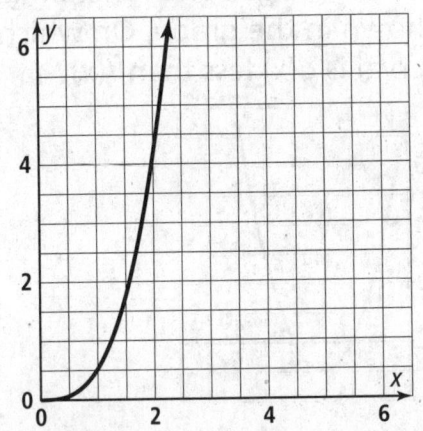

   Ⓐ Cube
   Ⓑ Sphere
   Ⓒ The volumes are equal.
   Ⓓ Impossible to tell

2. Function f is represented by the equation $f(x) = x^3 + 4x^2 - 7x - 10$. Function g is shown in the graph. Over which interval is $f(x) > g(x)$?

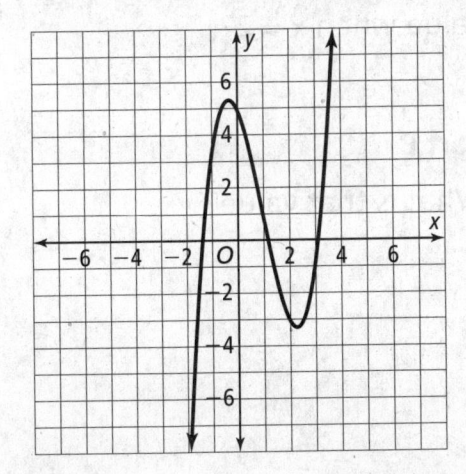

   Ⓐ [−5, −3]
   Ⓑ [−1, 1]
   Ⓒ [2, 5]
   Ⓓ [5, 8]

3. The graph of a linear function f passes through the points (2, 5) and (4, 7). Function g is represented by the equation $g(x) = 0.75x + 3$.

   Part A

   Which function has the greater slope?

   Part B

   What is that slope?

4. Function f is represented by the table. Function g is represented by the equation $g(x) = x^2 + 4x + 4$. Select each value of x where $f(x)$ is greater than $g(x)$.

x	f(x)
−5	8
−3	6
−1	4
1	2
3	0

   ☐ A. −5
   ☐ B. −3
   ☐ C. −1
   ☐ D. 1
   ☐ E. 3

5. The graph shows the function f. The function g is represented by the equation $g(x) = x^2 + 2x - 24$.

Which function is greater when x = 1? What is the value of the greater function?

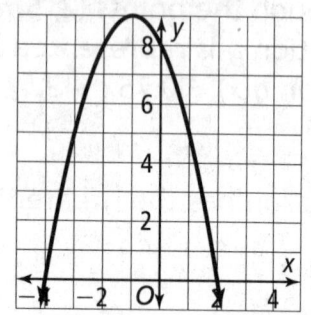

Ⓐ f; f(1) = 5
Ⓑ f; f(1) = 21
Ⓒ g; g(1) = 21
Ⓓ g; g(1) = −21

6. The function f is represented by the equation $f(x) = x^2 - 7x - 10$. The function g has a value equal to the square root of the sum of x and 4. Which function has the greater value when x = 5? What is that value?

Ⓐ f; f(5) = −20
Ⓑ f; f(5) = 3
Ⓒ g; g(5) = −20
Ⓓ g; g(5) = 3

7. Function f is represented by the graph. Function g is represented by the equation $g(x) = 0.5x + 2$. Select all values of x where f(x) is greater than g(x).

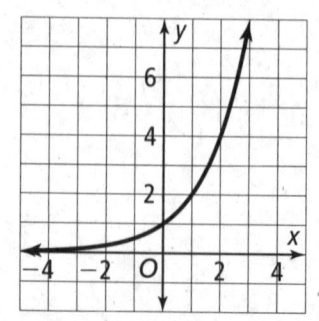

☐ A. −4
☐ B. −1
☐ C. 0
☐ D. 1
☐ E. 2

8. The value of f is the absolute value of the difference x minus 2. Let $g(x) = \frac{1}{3}x + 2$. Select all values of x where f(x) is greater than g(x).

☐ A. −3
☐ B. 0
☐ C. 2
☐ D. 5
☐ E. 7

9. Let $f(x) = 2 \log x$. The function g is shown in the graph. On which interval is g(x) less than f(x)?

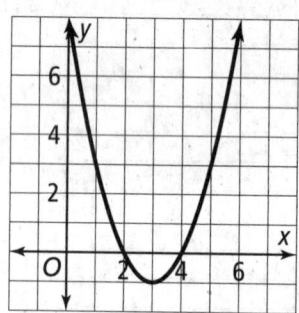

Ⓐ (0, 1]
Ⓑ [2, 4]
Ⓒ [5, 6]
Ⓓ [6, 7]

10. The graph of a linear function f passes through the points (−1, 1) and (0, −5). Function g is represented by the equation $g(x) = -x^3$.

Part A

Which function has the greater value when x = 2?

Part B

What is that value?

Common Core Standards Practice

HSF.BF.A.1

1. Rae is constructing an open box from a piece of paper that is 6 in. wide and 4.5 in. long. Rae cuts squares of equal size from each corner of the paper, and then folds up the sides of the box. Write and simplify a polynomial function V for the volume of the box in terms of x.

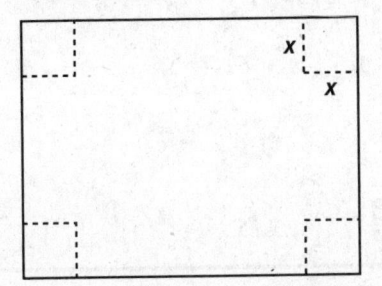

2. Let $f(x) = 2x - 7$. Identify the rule for $f(f(x)) - f(x)$.
   - Ⓐ $f(f(x)) - f(x) = 4x - 21$
   - Ⓑ $f(f(x)) - f(x) = 2x - 14$
   - Ⓒ $f(f(x)) - f(x) = 2x - 28$
   - Ⓓ $f(f(x)) - f(x) = 4x - 14$

3. Let $f(x) = 2x - 1$ and $g(x) = \frac{3}{x+1}$. Find $\frac{(f \cdot g)(1) + (g \cdot f)(1)}{(f \cdot f)(0)}$.

4. Let $f(x) = 2x^2 + x - 2$ and $g(x) = 3x + 2$. Identify the rule for $g(f(x)) + g(x)$.
   - Ⓐ $g(f(x)) + g(x) = 6x^2 + 6x - 2$
   - Ⓑ $g(f(x)) + g(x) = 6x^2 + 3x - 2$
   - Ⓒ $g(f(x)) + g(x) = 3x^2 + 6x - 4$
   - Ⓓ $g(f(x)) + g(x) = 2x^4 + 3x - 2$

5. Let $f(x) = \sqrt[3]{x - 1}$. Find $f(f(28))$.
   - Ⓐ 7
   - Ⓑ $\sqrt[3]{3}$
   - Ⓒ $\sqrt[3]{2}$
   - Ⓓ 3

6. Let $f(x) = \sqrt[3]{x + 1}$ and $g(x) = x^3$. Select all rules that are true.
   - ☐ A. $f(g(x)) + g(x) = x^3 + x + 1$
   - ☐ B. $g(f(x)) = x + 1$
   - ☐ C. $f(x) - f(g(x)) = \sqrt[3]{x + 1} - (x + 1)$
   - ☐ D. $g(f(x)) = \sqrt[3]{x^3 + 1}$
   - ☐ E. $g(f(x)) + f(g(x)) = x + 1 + \sqrt[3]{x^3 + 1}$

7. Let $f(x) = -x^2 + 1$ and $g(x) = \sqrt{x + 1}$. Select all rules that are true.
   - ☐ A. $(f \cdot g)(x) = x$
   - ☐ B. $(g \cdot f)(x) + f(x) = -x + \sqrt{2} - x^2 + 1$
   - ☐ C. $(f \cdot g)(x) - f(x) = x^2 - x - 1$
   - ☐ D. $(g \cdot f)(x) = \sqrt{-x^2 + 2}$
   - ☐ E. $(f \cdot g)(x) - (g \cdot f)(x) = 0$

8. Let $f(x) = -x^2 + x$ and $g(x) = \sqrt{x+1}$. Identify the rule for $\dfrac{(f \cdot g)(3) + (g \cdot f)(0)}{(f \cdot f)(-1)}$.

  Ⓐ -3
  Ⓑ 0
  Ⓒ $-\dfrac{1}{6}$
  Ⓓ undefined

9. Let $f(x) = x^2 + 1$ and $g(x) = \sqrt{x-1}$. Identify the rule for $\dfrac{f(g(x))}{g(f(x))}$.

10. Let $f(x) = x^3 - 1$ and $g(x) = \sqrt[3]{x}$. Identify the rule for $\dfrac{f(x)}{g(f(x))}$.

  Ⓐ $\dfrac{f(x)}{g(f(x))} = \sqrt[3]{(x^3-1)^2}$
  Ⓑ $\dfrac{f(x)}{g(f(x))} = -1$
  Ⓒ $\dfrac{f(x)}{g(f(x))} = \dfrac{-1}{\sqrt[3]{x}-1}$
  Ⓓ $\dfrac{f(x)}{g(f(x))} = \dfrac{x^3-1}{x-1}$

11. The demand, d, for a product at cost x is given by the function $d(x) = 750 - 3x$, the price p in dollars that can be charged for the product is given by $p(x) = 2x + 3$ and the revenue function, $R(x)$, for this product is $R(x) = p(x) \times d(x)$. What is the revenue in dollars for a product that costs $5?

12. Let $f(x) = x^3$ and $g(x) = \sqrt[3]{x} - 1$. Find $\dfrac{f(g(-8)) + g(f(5))}{g(g(0))}$.

  Ⓐ $-\dfrac{31}{2}$
  Ⓑ $\dfrac{31}{2}$
  Ⓒ $\dfrac{23}{2}$
  Ⓓ $-\dfrac{23}{2}$

13. Let $f(x) = 2\log x$ and $g(x) = 10^x$. Select all rules that are true.

  ☐ A. $f(x) + g(x) = 20\log x$
  ☐ B. $f(x) - g(x) = 2\log x - 10^x$
  ☐ C. $(f \circ g)(x) = 2x$
  ☐ D. $(f \circ g)(x) - (g \circ f)(x) = 2x - 10$
  ☐ E. $(f \circ g)(x) - g(x) = 2x - 10^x$

Name _____

Common Core Standards Practice

HSF.BF.B.3

1. Select all the transformations of $f(x) = x^2$ that combine to result in the graph of function g, below.

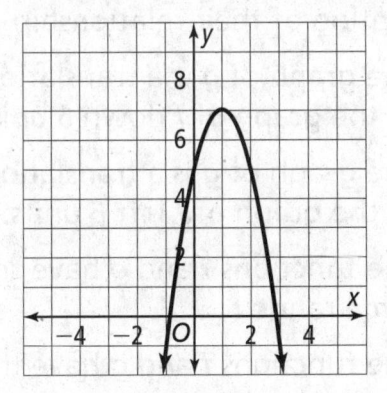

   ☐ A. translation of 1 unit left and 7 units down
   ☐ B. translation of 1 unit right and 7 units up
   ☐ C. horizontal stretch by a factor of 2
   ☐ D. vertical stretch by a factor of 2
   ☐ E. reflection across the x-axis

2. The function $g(x) = \frac{1}{3}(x - 2)^2 + 5$ is a transformation of the parent function $f(x) = x^2$. Select all the transformations performed on function f to produce function g.

   ☐ A. translate f 2 units left
   ☐ B. translate f 2 units right
   ☐ C. translate f 5 units up
   ☐ D. compress f vertically by a factor of 3
   ☐ E. stretch f vertically by a factor of 3

3. Which steps transform the graph of $y = x^2$ into the graph of $y = \frac{1}{2}(x - 1)^2 + 3$?

   Ⓐ Compress horizontally by a factor of 2; translate 1 unit to the left and 3 units up.
   Ⓑ Compress vertically by a factor of 2; translate 1 unit to the right and 3 units up.
   Ⓒ Compress vertically by a factor of 2; translate 3 units to the right and 1 unit down.
   Ⓓ Compress horizontally by a factor of 2; translate 1 unit to the right and 3 units up.

4. Function g is a transformation of the parent function $f(x) = x^2$. The graph of g is reflected across the x-axis, then translated right 2 units and up 5 units from the graph of f. What is the equation of function g written in standard form?

5. The graph of $y = x^2 - 5x + 1$ is reflected across the x-axis and then translated down 5 units.

   What is an equation of the transformed graph?

   Ⓐ $y = x^2 + 5x - 4$
   Ⓑ $y = -x^2 + 5x - 6$
   Ⓒ $y = -x^2 - 5x - 4$
   Ⓓ $y = -x^2 + 5x + 4$

6. Determine the equation of the cubic or quartic function f, represented by the graph below.

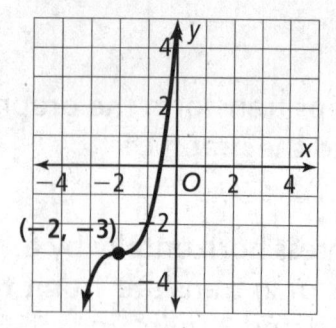

7. Select the function f(x) shown in the graph.

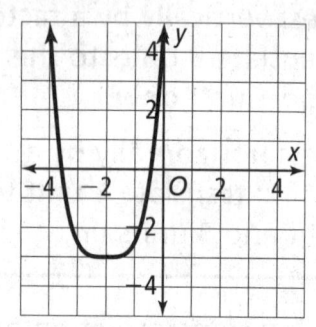

   Ⓐ $f(x) = \frac{1}{2}(x+2)^4 - 3$
   Ⓑ $f(x) = \frac{1}{2}(x-2)^4 - 3$
   Ⓒ $f(x) = 2(x+2)^4 - 3$
   Ⓓ $f(x) = 2(x-3)^4 - 2$

8. The logarithmic function $f(x) = \log x$ is transformed to $g(x) = \log(x-2) + 1$. Which of the following are true? Select all true statements.

   ☐ A. f(x) is shifted 2 units down.
   ☐ B. f(x) is shifted 1 unit up.
   ☐ C. f(x) is shifted 2 units up.
   ☐ D. f(x) is shifted 2 units right.
   ☐ E. f(x) is shifted 2 units left.

9. The graph of $g(x) = \sqrt{x} - 2$ is a translation of what parent function?

10. The function $g(x) = \sqrt{x-6}$ is a transformation of the parent function $f(x) = \sqrt{x}$. Select the best description of their relationship.

    Ⓐ The graph of g is a translation of the graph of f down 6 units.
    Ⓑ The graph of g is a translation of the graph of f left 6 units.
    Ⓒ The functions f and g have the same range.
    Ⓓ The functions f and g have the same domain.

11. Which function represents the exponential function $f(x) = -2^x$ after a vertical stretch by a factor of 4 and a reflection across the x-axis?

    Ⓐ $f(x) = -4^x$
    Ⓑ $f(x) = -2^{x+2}$
    Ⓒ $f(x) = 4^x$
    Ⓓ $f(x) = 2^{x+2}$

12. The graph of $y = x^3$ is translated 5 units down and 7 units to the left. What is an equation of the translated graph?

    Ⓐ $y = (x-7)^2 - 5$
    Ⓑ $y = (x+7)^3 - 5$
    Ⓒ $y = (x-5)^3 + 7$
    Ⓓ $y = (x+7)^3 + 5$

Common Core Standards Practice

HSF.BF.B.4

1. Write the inverse of the function $f(x) = \left(\frac{1}{2}\right)^{x-1}$.

2. Is each function one-to-one?

	Yes	No
$f(x) = \frac{1}{2}x^3 - 3$	☐	☐
$f(x) = \sqrt{8x}$	☐	☐
$f(x) = x^2 + 4$	☐	☐

3. Write the inverse of the function $f(x) = (x-2)^3 + 1$.

4. Are each pair of functions f and g inverses of each other, on their domains?

	Yes	No
$f(x) = 3x + 9$ and $g(x) = x - 3$	☐	☐
$f(x) = 2x - 6$ and $g(x) = \frac{1}{2}x + 3$	☐	☐
$f(x) = x^2 + 1$ and $g(x) = \sqrt{x} - 1$	☐	☐

5. Let $f(x) = x^2 + 2x + 1$. Find the inverse function f by identifying an appropriate restriction of its domain.

   Ⓐ The inverse is $f^{-1}(x) = \sqrt{x} - 1$, for $x \geq -1$.

   Ⓑ The inverse is $f^{-1}(x) = \sqrt{x} - 1$, for $x \geq 1$.

   Ⓒ The inverse is $f^{-1}(x) = \sqrt{x} + 1$, for $x \geq 0$.

   Ⓓ The function does not have an inverse.

6. Find the values of a and b such that the functions $f(x) = ax - 4$ and $g(x) = 2x + b$ are inverses of each other on their domains.

   ☐ A. $a = \frac{1}{2}$

   ☐ B. $a = -2$

   ☐ C. $b = -4$

   ☐ D. $b = 4$

   ☐ E. $b = 8$

7. Find an equation of the inverse of the function $f(x) = 2\sqrt[3]{x-1} + 1$.

   Ⓐ $f^{-1}(x) = \frac{1}{4}(x-1)^2 - 1$

   Ⓑ $f^{-1}(x) = \frac{1}{2}(x-1)^3 + 1$

   Ⓒ $f^{-1}(x) = \frac{1}{8}(x-1)^3 + 1$

   Ⓓ $f^{-1}(x) = \frac{1}{8}(x+1)^3 - 1$

8. Let $f(x) = x^2 - 4x + 4$. Find the inverse function f by identifying an appropriate restriction of its domain.

   Ⓐ The inverse is $f^{-1}(x) = \sqrt{x} - 2$, for $x \geq -2$.

   Ⓑ The inverse is $f^{-1}(x) = \sqrt{x+2}$, for $x \geq 2$.

   Ⓒ The inverse is $f^{-1}(x) = \sqrt{x} + 2$, for $x \geq 2$.

   Ⓓ The function does not have an inverse.

9. The table shows the inverse of a function f. What is the value of $f(-3)$?

x	-7	-3	2	4	5
$f^{-1}(x)$	0	-1	2	-2	-3

10. Write the inverse of the function $f(x) = \sqrt[3]{2x+4} - 2$.

11. Find the values of a and b such that the functions $f(x) = 2x^2 - b$ and $g(x) = \sqrt{ax+2}$ are inverses of each other on their domains.

    ☐ A. $a = \frac{1}{2}$
    ☐ B. $a = -2$
    ☐ C. $a = 4$
    ☐ D. $b = 4$
    ☐ E. $b = 2$

12. Let $f(x) = 2\sqrt{x-3}$. Find the inverse function f and identify an appropriate restriction of its domain.

    ☐ A. $f^{-1}(x) = \frac{1}{2}x^2 + 3$
    ☐ B. $f^{-1}(x) = 2x^2 + 3$
    ☐ C. $f^{-1}(x) = \frac{1}{4}x^2 + 3$
    ☐ D. $x \geq 3$
    ☐ E. $x \geq 0$

13. Which function is the inverse of the exponential function $y = 7^x$?

    Ⓐ $y = \log_7 x$
    Ⓑ $y = \left(\frac{1}{7}\right)^x$
    Ⓒ $y = x^{-7}$
    Ⓓ $y = 7^{-x}$

14. Which function is the inverse of the exponential function $y = 2.5^x$?

    Ⓐ $y = 2x^{-5}$
    Ⓑ $y = \frac{1}{2} \cdot 5^{-x}$
    Ⓒ $y = \log_{2.5} x$
    Ⓓ $y = 2\left(\frac{1}{5}\right)^x$

15. Find an expression for the inverse of the function $f(x) = \log_5(0.5x)$.

    Ⓐ $f^{-1}(x) = 0.5(5)^x$
    Ⓑ $f^{-1}(x) = 5^x$
    Ⓒ $f^{-1}(x) = 2(5)^x$
    Ⓓ $f^{-1}(x) = 5(0.5)^x$

16. Find an expression for the inverse of the function $f(x) = \log_3(8x)$.

    Ⓐ $f^{-1}(x) = \frac{1}{8} \cdot 3^x$
    Ⓑ $f^{-1}(x) = 3^x$
    Ⓒ $f^{-1}(x) = 8 \cdot 3^x$
    Ⓓ $f^{-1}(x) = 3 \cdot 8^x$

Name _____

Common Core Standards Practice

HSF.LE.A.4

enVision Algebra 2

SavvasRealize.com

1. Write the logarithmic equation $\log_7 49 = 2$ in exponential form.
   - Ⓐ $2^{49} = 7$
   - Ⓑ $49^2 = 7$
   - Ⓒ $7^2 = 49$
   - Ⓓ $2^7 = 49$

2. What is the solution to the equation $\log(3x + 1) = 2$?
   - Ⓐ $x = \frac{1}{3}$
   - Ⓑ $x = 3$
   - Ⓒ $x = 33$
   - Ⓓ $x = 100$

3. Write the logarithmic equation that is equivalent to the exponential form $5^2 = 25$.
   - Ⓐ $\log_5 25 = 2$
   - Ⓑ $\log_2 25 = 5$
   - Ⓒ $\log_2 5 = 25$
   - Ⓓ $\log_{25} 5 = 2$

4. Write the logarithmic equation $\log_5 125 = 3$ in exponential form.
   - Ⓐ $125^5 = 3$
   - Ⓑ $125^3 = 5$
   - Ⓒ $3^5 = 125$
   - Ⓓ $5^3 = 125$

5. What is the solution to the equation $\log(4x - 8) = 2$?
   - Ⓐ $x = \frac{5}{2}$
   - Ⓑ $x = 23$
   - Ⓒ $x = 27$
   - Ⓓ $x = 100$

6. A small company uses this function to relate sales revenue R and expenses, C, both in thousands of dollars:

   $R = 8 \log(C + 1) + 36$

   If their revenue last year was $48,000, what were their expenses? Round your answer to the nearest dollar.

7. Select all the logarithmic expressions that have been evaluated correctly, to the nearest hundredth.
   - ☐ A. $\log_4 16 = 2$
   - ☐ B. $\log_4 12 = 1.79$
   - ☐ C. $\log_4 9 = 1.92$
   - ☐ D. $\log_4 64 = 4$
   - ☐ E. $\log_4 11 = 2.11$

8. Use the Change of Base Formula to solve the equation $2^x = 6$ for x. Give an exact solution as a logarithm, and an approximate solution rounded to the nearest thousandth.

---

9. Find the solution of the equation $3^{2x+1} = 7$.

   Ⓐ $x = \dfrac{\log 7}{\log 3} - 0.5$

   Ⓑ $x = \dfrac{\log 7}{2 \log 3} + 0.5$

   Ⓒ $x = \dfrac{\log 7}{\log 3} + 0.5$

   Ⓓ $x = \dfrac{\log 7}{2 \log 3} - 0.5$

---

10. Use the Change of Base Formula to solve the equation $3^x = 5$ for x. Give an exact solution as a logarithm, and an approximate solution rounded to the nearest thousandth.

---

11. Select all the logarithmic expressions that have been evaluated correctly, to the nearest hundredth.

    ☐ A. $\log_3 12 = 2.26$
    ☐ B. $\log_2 16 = 3.51$
    ☐ C. $\log_5 12 = 1.54$
    ☐ D. $\log_7 49 = -2$
    ☐ E. $\log_5 15 = 1.68$

---

12. Select which function has the greatest value at each of the given x-values.

	−5	−2	4	5
$f(x) = 2x + 8$	☐	☐	☐	☐
$g(x) = x^2 + 3x - 5$	☐	☐	☐	☐
$h(x) = 4^{x-2}$	☐	☐	☐	☐

---

13. A quadratic function f models the predicted profit, in thousands of dollars, for a company M after x years. An exponential function g models the predicted profit, for a company N. Find the average rate of change for each function from $x = 2$ to $x = 4$.

Which company has the greater average rate of change of its profit over that interval?

x	f(x)	g(x)
1	4	6
2	5	9
3	7	21
4	13	69

☐ A. f: $4,000 per year, g: $30,000 per year

☐ B. f: $2,600 per year, g: $7,667 per year

☐ C. f: $7,500 per year, g: $133 per year

☐ D. Company N has a greater average rate of change.

☐ E. Company M has a greater average rate of change.

Common Core Standards Practice

HSF.TF.A.1, HSF.TF.A.2

1. The arc length subtended by an angle on a circle of radius 4 is 2π. What is the radian measure of the angle?
   - Ⓐ $\frac{\pi}{4}$
   - Ⓑ $\frac{\pi}{2}$
   - Ⓒ π
   - Ⓓ 2π

2. The arc length subtended by an angle on a circle of radius 15 is 5π. What is the radian measure of the angle?
   - Ⓐ $\frac{\pi}{15}$
   - Ⓑ $\frac{\pi}{5}$
   - Ⓒ $\frac{\pi}{3}$
   - Ⓓ 3π

3. The angle θ corresponds to the arc length $\frac{3\pi}{4}$ on the unit circle. What is the measure of θ in degrees?
   - Ⓐ 22.5
   - Ⓑ 45
   - Ⓒ 135
   - Ⓓ 270

4. The angle θ has radian measure $\frac{2\pi}{5}$. What is the measure of θ in degrees?
   - Ⓐ 36
   - Ⓑ 40
   - Ⓒ 72
   - Ⓓ 144

5. The degree measure of angle θ is 20°. What is the radian measure of θ?
   - Ⓐ $\frac{\pi}{20}$
   - Ⓑ $\frac{\pi}{18}$
   - Ⓒ $\frac{\pi}{9}$
   - Ⓓ $\frac{2\pi}{9}$

Use the figure for items 6 and 7.

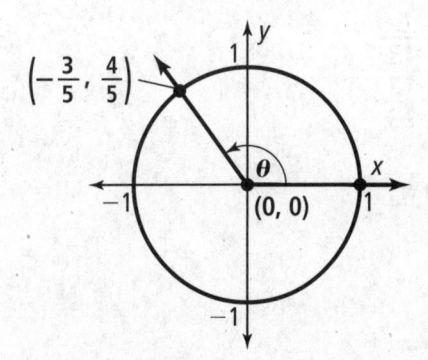

6. What is $\sin\theta$?
   - Ⓐ $-\frac{4}{5}$
   - Ⓑ $-\frac{3}{5}$
   - Ⓒ $\frac{3}{5}$
   - Ⓓ $\frac{4}{5}$

7. What is $\tan\theta$?
   - Ⓐ $-\frac{4}{3}$
   - Ⓑ $-\frac{3}{4}$
   - Ⓒ $\frac{3}{4}$
   - Ⓓ $\frac{4}{3}$

8. Angle θ in standard position has a terminal ray that passes through the point (8, −6). What is sin θ?

   Ⓐ $-\frac{4}{5}$

   Ⓑ $-\frac{3}{5}$

   Ⓒ $\frac{3}{5}$

   Ⓓ $\frac{4}{5}$

9. Angle θ in standard position has a terminal ray that passes through the point (−12, −5). What is cos θ?

   Ⓐ $-\frac{12}{13}$

   Ⓑ $-\frac{5}{13}$

   Ⓒ $\frac{5}{13}$

   Ⓓ $\frac{12}{13}$

10. Angle θ in standard position has a terminal ray that passes through the point (−2, 7). What is tan θ?

    Ⓐ $-\frac{7}{2}$

    Ⓑ $-\frac{2}{7}$

    Ⓒ $\frac{2}{7}$

    Ⓓ $\frac{7}{2}$

Common Core Standards Practice

HSF.TF.B.5

1. Which equation is represented by the graph?

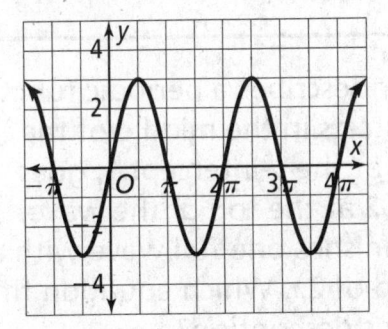

    Ⓐ $y = -3 \sin x$
    Ⓑ $y = -3 \cos x$
    Ⓒ $y = 3 \sin x$
    Ⓓ $y = 3 \cos x$

2. Julie describes a periodic function that starts at the peak of the wave at the y-intercept 9, goes down to 7 at the bottom of the wave, and finishes one full wave with a period of 2π. Which equation fits Julie's description?

    Ⓐ $y = \sin x + 9$
    Ⓑ $y = \cos x + 9$
    Ⓒ $y = \sin x + 8$
    Ⓓ $y = \cos x + 8$

3. Which function has a period of $\frac{\pi}{2}$?

    Ⓐ $y = \sin \frac{x}{4}$
    Ⓑ $y = \sin \frac{x}{2}$
    Ⓒ $y = \sin 2x$
    Ⓓ $y = \sin 4x$

4. Write an equation is represented by the graph.

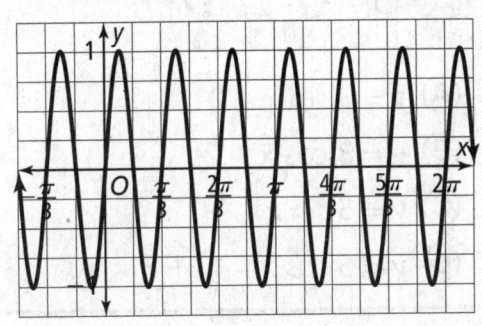

5. Dinah describes a periodic function that starts in the middle of the wave at the y-intercept 0, goes up to 4 at the top of the wave, and finishes one full wave with a period of 2π. Which equation fits Dinah's description?

    Ⓐ $y = 4 \sin x$
    Ⓑ $y = 4 \cos x$
    Ⓒ $y = \sin x + 4$
    Ⓓ $y = \cos x + 4$

6. Which function has a midline of 5?

    Ⓐ $y = 5 \sin x$
    Ⓑ $y = \sin \frac{x}{2} + 5$
    Ⓒ $y = \sin 5x$
    Ⓓ $y = 10 \sin \frac{x}{5}$

7. Which equation is represented by the graph?

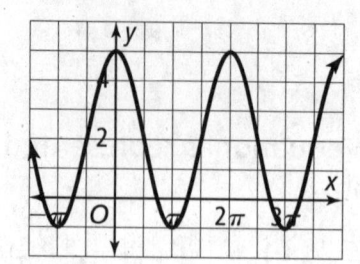

Ⓐ $y = 3 \sin x + 2$
Ⓑ $y = 3 \cos x + 2$
Ⓒ $y = 5 \sin x - 1$
Ⓓ $y = 5 \cos x - 1$

8. Mei describes a periodic function that starts at the peak of the wave at the y-intercept −1, goes down to −3 at the bottom of the wave, and finishes one full wave with a period of π. Which equation fits Mei's description?

Ⓐ $y = \sin 2x - 1$
Ⓑ $y = 2 \cos x - 2$
Ⓒ $y = 2 \sin \frac{x}{2} - 1$
Ⓓ $y = \cos 2x - 1$

9. Which function has an amplitude of 3 and a period of 6?

Ⓐ $y = 3 \sin 6\pi x$
Ⓑ $y = 6 \sin \frac{\pi x}{6} + 5$
Ⓒ $y = 6 \sin 3\pi x$
Ⓓ $y = 3 \sin \frac{\pi x}{3}$

10. Taylor describes a periodic function that starts in the middle of the wave at the y-intercept 1, goes up to 2 at the top of the wave, and finishes one full wave with a period of 2π. Which equation fits Taylor's description?

Ⓐ $y = \sin 2x + 1$
Ⓑ $y = 2 \cos x - 1$
Ⓒ $y = \sin x + 1$
Ⓓ $y = \cos 2x - 1$

Common Core Standards Practice

HSF.TF.C.8

1. Complete the proof below to prove $\sin^2 \theta + \cos^2 \theta = 1$.

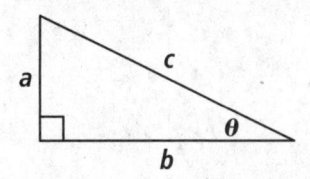

   Given: A right triangle with leg lengths a and b and hypotenuse length c, and angle θ opposite the side of length a.

   Prove: $\sin^2 \theta + \cos^2 \theta = 1$

Statement	Reason
A right triangle with leg lengths a and b and hypotenuse length c, and angle θ opposite the side of length a.	Given
$a^2 + b^2 = c^2$	
$\frac{a^2}{c^2} + \frac{b^2}{c^2} = \frac{c^2}{c^2}$	
$\left(\frac{a}{c}\right)^2 + \left(\frac{b}{c}\right)^2 = 1$	Division Property of Exponents
$\sin^2 \theta + \cos^2 \theta = 1$	Definitions of _____ and _____

2. Given $\sin \theta = \frac{3}{5}$ and θ is in Quadrant I, what is $\cos \theta$?

   Ⓐ $-\frac{4}{5}$
   Ⓑ $-\frac{3}{5}$
   Ⓒ $\frac{3}{5}$
   Ⓓ $\frac{4}{5}$

3. Given $\sin \theta = \frac{4}{5}$ and θ is in Quadrant II, what is $\tan \theta$?

   Ⓐ $-\frac{4}{3}$
   Ⓑ $-\frac{3}{4}$
   Ⓒ $\frac{3}{4}$
   Ⓓ $\frac{4}{3}$

4. Given $\cos \theta = -\frac{5}{13}$ and θ is in Quadrant III, what is $\sin \theta$?

   Ⓐ $-\frac{12}{13}$
   Ⓑ $-\frac{5}{13}$
   Ⓒ $\frac{5}{13}$
   Ⓓ $\frac{12}{15}$

5. Given $\cos \theta = \frac{12}{13}$ and θ is in Quadrant IV, what is $\tan \theta$?

   Ⓐ $-\frac{12}{5}$
   Ⓑ $-\frac{5}{12}$
   Ⓒ $\frac{5}{12}$
   Ⓓ $\frac{12}{5}$

6. Given $\cos \theta = \frac{8}{17}$ and θ is in Quadrant I, what is $\tan \theta$?

   Ⓐ $-\frac{15}{8}$
   Ⓑ $-\frac{8}{15}$
   Ⓒ $\frac{8}{15}$
   Ⓓ $\frac{15}{8}$

7. Given $\cos \theta = -\frac{15}{17}$ and θ is in Quadrant II, what is $\sin \theta$?
   - Ⓐ $-\frac{15}{17}$
   - Ⓑ $-\frac{8}{17}$
   - Ⓒ $\frac{8}{17}$
   - Ⓓ $\frac{15}{17}$

8. Given $\sin \theta = -0.8$ and θ is in Quadrant III, what is $\cos \theta$?

9. Given $\sin \theta = -0.6$ and θ is in Quadrant IV, what is $\tan \theta$?

10. Given $\tan \theta = \frac{4}{3}$ and θ is in Quadrant III, what is $\cos \theta$?
    - Ⓐ $-\frac{4}{5}$
    - Ⓑ $-\frac{3}{5}$
    - Ⓒ $\frac{3}{5}$
    - Ⓓ $\frac{4}{5}$

Common Core Standards Practice

HSS.ID.A.4

A data set with a mean of 47 and a standard deviation of 3.15 is normally distributed. Use this information for Items 1–3.

1. Use the Emprical Rule to match each range to the approximate percent of data that falls within it.

Range	84%	97.5%	81.5%
Between 40.7 and 50.15	☐	☐	☐
Greater than 43.85	☐	☐	☐
Less than 53.3	☐	☐	☐

2. Select the data value that best matches each statement.

Data Value	Greater than approximately 83% of the distribution	Less than approximately 9.25% of the distribution
40	☐	☐
42	☐	☐
44	☐	☐
46	☐	☐

3. What percent of values have the following z-scores?

   $0.5 \leq z \leq 1.00$

4. Given the mean $\mu = 34$ and standard deviation $\sigma = 2.4$, find the z-score for data point $x = 12$. Round to nearest hundredth if necessary.

_____

5. A data set is normally distributed with mean 70 and standard deviation 1.3. Approximately what percent of the data are greater than 68.7?

   Ⓐ 16%
   Ⓑ 68%
   Ⓒ 84%
   Ⓓ 95%

6. A data set is normally distributed with a mean of 17.4 and a standard deviation of 0.8. Find the z-score for a value of 20.1, to the nearest hundredth.

   Ⓐ −3.38
   Ⓑ −1.11
   Ⓒ 1.11
   Ⓓ 3.38

7. An automobile safety rating system has a mean score of 100 with a standard deviation of 7.6. A new car receives a rating of 118. Which statement best describes the safety rating of the new car?

   Ⓐ The new car's rating is more than 3 standard deviations from the mean.

   Ⓑ The new car's rating is higher than 97.5% of all cars tested.

   Ⓒ The z-score for the new car is approximately −2.37.

   Ⓓ The new car's rating is higher than 99.7% of all cars tested.

8. In a data set with a normal distribution, the mean is 64 and the standard deviation is 4

   Part A

   About what percent of the data lie between 52 and 68?

   Ⓐ 68% Ⓒ 81.5%

   Ⓑ 83.85% Ⓓ 50%

   Part B

   Determine which of the following is NOT true about the normal distribution.

   Ⓐ About 68% of the data lie between 60 and 68.

   Ⓑ About 68% of the data lie between 60 and 68.

   Ⓒ About 47.5% of the data lie between 60 and 64.

   Ⓓ About 81.5% of the data lie between 56 and 68.

9. A data set is normally distributed, with a mean of 52 and standard deviation of 6. About 95% of the data lie between which two values?

   ☐ A. 40
   ☐ B. 42
   ☐ C. 50
   ☐ D. 62
   ☐ E. 64

10. A data set is normally distributed, with a mean of 82 and standard deviation of 4. About 90% of the data lie between which two values?

    ☐ A. 72
    ☐ B. 74
    ☐ C. 75
    ☐ D. 89
    ☐ E. 90

11. A data set is normally distributed, with a mean of 38 and standard deviation of 7. About 95% of the data lie between which two values?

    ☐ A. 24
    ☐ B. 26
    ☐ C. 50
    ☐ D. 52
    ☐ E. 56

12. In the United States, men's heights have a mean of 70 inches and a standard deviation of 3 inches. Find the z-score for a height of 76 inches.

Common Core Standards Practice

HSS.IC.A.1, HSS.IC.A.2

Use the information for items 1–3.

The student council at a school with 1,530 students wants to survey the students to find out what kind of end of year activity they want to have. The council members surveyed the 258 students in their homerooms.

1. Did the survey give an accurate representation of student opinions? Select the true statement.

    Ⓐ No; the survey is too small.

    Ⓑ No; the survey did not randomly select students.

    Ⓒ Yes; the sample was sufficiently large and representative of the population.

    Ⓓ Yes; students enjoyed the picnic.

2. How large is the population of the survey?

    Ⓐ 16.8
    Ⓑ 258
    Ⓒ 1,272
    Ⓓ 1,530

3. How large is the sample of the survey?

    Ⓐ 16.8
    Ⓑ 258
    Ⓒ 1,272
    Ⓓ 1,530

4. A town surveys 400 households and finds that the households have on average 2.3 pets. Later the town is able to ask every one of the 17,150 households how many pets they have, and the average is 2.1 pets. What is the size of the population in this survey?

5. A company sales manager surveys 400 customers and the average number of items bought in a year is 28.6 items. Later a company data analyst computes the average number of items bought in a year by all 418,913 customers, which is 31.4 items. What is the size of the parameter in this survey?

6. A student asks 100 people in her town whether they will vote for Candidate A in the upcoming election, and 57% say yes. In the election, 3,953 people vote, and Candidate A receives 51.8% of the votes. What is the size of the sample in this survey?

7. Darcy opens 24 packs of trading cards and finds that 7.9% of the cards are rare. The trading card company website says that of the 2,000,000 packs they sold last year, 10% of the cards were rare cards. What is the size of the statistic in this survey?

---

8. Tomiko flips a coin 10 times and it comes up heads 8 times. She thinks that if there is less than a 5% chance that a fair coin will give 8 or more heads out of 10 flips, her coin is not fair. Tomiko simulates flipping a fair coin 100 times and records the number of heads with the following results.

Heads	0	1	2	3	4	5	6	7	8	9	10
Frequency	0	1	3	15	24	25	18	11	2	1	0

What is the estimate of the probability of 8 or more heads in Tomiko's simulation, and does she consider that her coin is fair?

Ⓐ 1%, not fair
Ⓑ 2%, not fair
Ⓒ 3%, not fair
Ⓓ 14%, fair

9. Javier rolls a six-sided die four times, and each time it comes up 6. He thinks that if there is less than a 1% chance that a fair die will come up 6 every time with four rolls, his die is not fair. What is the probability that a fair die will come up 6 every time out of four rolls, and does Javier consider that his coin is fair?

Ⓐ 0.08%, not fair
Ⓑ 0.5%, not fair
Ⓒ 2.8%, fair
Ⓓ 16.7%, fair

---

10. Darius opened a pack of 10 trading cards and 3 of them were special cards. The company website says that 10% of the cards are special cards. Darius simulates opening 150 packs of trading cards and decides that if 3% or less of the simulations have 3 or more special cards, the company website is incorrect. What is Darius' estimate of the probability that a pack has 3 or more cards, and does he think the website is correct?

Special Cards	0	1	2	3
Frequency	36	74	35	5

Ⓐ 0.03%, not correct
Ⓑ 3%, not correct
Ⓒ 3.3%, correct
Ⓓ 5%, correct

Name _____

Common Core Standards Practice

HSS.IC.B.3

1. A teacher decides to give her students an experimental quiz. Which statement is true?

    Ⓐ She should give all of her students the quiz and compare their results to last year's quiz.

    Ⓑ She should give her morning class the experimental quiz and the afternoon class the usual quiz.

    Ⓒ She should give her morning class the usual quiz and the afternoon class the experimental quiz.

    Ⓓ She should randomly choose half of her students to take the experimental quiz and the other half to take the usual quiz.

2. Po wants to know whether students at his school like algebra or geometry better. What kind of study should he do?

    Ⓐ experiment
    Ⓑ observational study
    Ⓒ sample survey
    Ⓓ study group

3. Maria wants to know whether letting students talk in study hall helps their grades. What kind of study should she do?

    Ⓐ experiment
    Ⓑ observational study
    Ⓒ sample survey
    Ⓓ study group

4. James and Clarissa are assigned a project to study the heights of students at their school. James randomly chooses a group of students and asks their heights. Clarissa measures the height of students in her classes. Which statements are true? Select all that apply.

    ☐ A. James conducted a sample survey.

    ☐ B. Clarissa conducted a sample survey.

    ☐ C. James conducted an observational study.

    ☐ D. Clarissa conducted an observational study.

    ☐ E. James' sample is likely to accurately reflect the population.

    ☐ F. Clarissa's sample is likely to accurately reflect the population.

    ☐ G. The way James collected his data is likely to give accurate measurements.

    ☐ H. The way Clarissa collected her data is likely to give accurate measurements.

5. Priya wants to know the average wrist circumference of students at her school. What kind of study should she do?

    Ⓐ experiment
    Ⓑ observational study
    Ⓒ sample survey
    Ⓓ study group

6. David wants to know if attending a study group helps students' grades. Which of the following should he do, if possible?

    ☐ A. Randomly choose students to take part in his study.
    ☐ B. Find out which students are already in study groups and compare them to students who aren't already in a group.
    ☐ C. Randomly assign students to attend a study group or attend a quiet study hall.
    ☐ D. Put all the students in his study in a study group.
    ☐ E. Choose whether a student will be in a study group based on whether their availability is convenient for him.
    ☐ F. For students assigned to be in a study group, assign them a group randomly.

7. Dwayne notices whether students at his school buy a hot lunch or bring a cold lunch. What kind of study is he doing?

    Ⓐ experiment
    Ⓑ observational study
    Ⓒ sample survey
    Ⓓ study group

8. Tomas and Shaniya are assigned a project to study whether using flash cards help students get better grades. Shaniya randomly chooses a group of students and asks them if they think using flash cards will help their grades. Tomas uses flash cards with the students in his French class that he knows and compares their quiz grades with the grades of the students he doesn't know. Which statements are true? Select all that apply.

    ☐ A. Tomas conducted a sample survey.
    ☐ B. Shaniya conducted a sample survey.
    ☐ C. Tomas conducted an observational study.
    ☐ D. Shaniya conducted an experiment.
    ☐ E. Tomas' sample is likely to accurately reflect the population.
    ☐ F. Shaniya's sample is likely to accurately reflect the population.
    ☐ G. The way Tomas collected his data is likely to give accurate measurements.
    ☐ H. The way Shaniya collected her data is likely to give accurate measurements.

Common Core Standards Practice

HSS.IC.B.4, HSS.IC.B.5

1. Ella randomly chooses 48 students at her school and asks them whether they have a cat as a pet, and 13 students say yes. Based on Ella's data, estimate the proportion of kids at her school that have a cat as a pet.

2. Izzy randomly chooses 20 students at her school and asks them how many pets they have. Based on Izzy's data, estimate the mean number of pets that students at her school have.

1	3	4	1	2	2	4	0	2	1
0	3	2	1	2	1	2	3	3	3

3. Darius wants to find the margin of error for his study where he asked 50 randomly selected students at his school whether the school should buy new sports equipment and 27 said yes. Which method will simulate his study?

   Ⓐ Flip a fair coin 50 times and see if there are 27 heads or more.

   Ⓑ Use a computer program 50 times to choose a random number between 0 and 100 and record how many times it is 27 or less.

   Ⓒ Use a computer program 50 times to choose a random number between 0 and 100 and record how many times it is 54 or less.

   Ⓓ Use a computer program 100 times to choose a random number between 0 and 50 and record how many times it is 54 or less.

4. Dakota wants to find the margin of error for a study where she asked 25 randomly selected students at her school whether they think the school should do away with homework and 21 said yes. She simulates her study 20 times with the results below. Dakota decides she wants the margin of error of the proportion of students at her school who want to do away with homework to be 0.04. What percentage of her simulated results have a difference of the margin of error or less of Dakota's sample proportion?

   23 21 20 19 22 21 21 20
   22 20 22 22 19 20 23 20
   24 19 19 20

   Ⓐ 65%   Ⓒ 95%
   Ⓑ 84%   Ⓓ 100%

5. Khadijah wants to find the margin of error for her study where she asked 40 randomly selected students at her school whether the school should add a salad bar and 13 said yes. She simulates her study 20 times with the results below. What margin of error proportion will include exactly 90% of the simulated results within the margin of error or less of Khadijah's sample proportion?

   11 11 13 13 10 14 14 16
   23 10 11 16 9 16 19 12 9
   13 9 15

   Ⓐ 0.05   Ⓒ 0.2
   Ⓑ 0.1   Ⓓ 0.25

6. A computer company found that on average households have 7.3 screens. They ran 20 simulations of their study and sorted the means from smallest to largest. Which margin of error will be greater than or equal to the difference between exactly 95% of the simulated means and the sample mean?

7.15 7.16 7.18 7.21 7.25 7.26
7.26 7.27 7.28 7.30 7.30 7.32
7.33 7.35 7.36 7.36 7.40 7.40
7.40 7.44

Ⓐ 0.019
Ⓑ 0.14
Ⓒ 0.15
Ⓓ 1.4

7. Asim wants to know if a plant food will help his plants grow taller. He grows 20 plants and randomly chooses 10 of them to get the new food and the rest to get the old food. The mean height of the plants getting the new food is 4 in. greater than the mean height of the plants getting the old food. Asim runs 100 simulations and puts the difference between the mean of the experimental group mean and the control group mean for each simulation in a table. What proportion of simulation means are 4 in. or greater?

Differences in Means (in.)	−5	−4	−3	−2	−1	0	1	2	3	4	5	6
Frequency	2	4	5	12	18	11	25	12	7	3	0	1

Ⓐ 0.01
Ⓑ 0.03
Ⓒ 0.04
Ⓓ 0.10

8. Yiwei measures her vertical jump 8 times with her new sneakers and her old sneakers. She records her data in a table. How much higher is her mean jump with the new sneakers?

New Sneakers (in.)	15.6	14.9	11.7	15.5	12.6	13.1	14.3	13.1
Old Sneakers (in.)	12.9	12.2	12.2	12.4	11.2	12.1	12.7	10.7

Ⓐ 0.9 in
Ⓑ 1.2 in.
Ⓒ 1.8 in.
Ⓓ 2.7 in.

9. Sylvia wants to perform simulations for her study where she fed 12 cats a commercial food and 12 cats a special diet, then measured the cats' weight loss. Which method will accurately simulate the control and experimental groups in her study?

Ⓐ Flip a fair coin for each cat. If it is heads, put the cat in the simulated experimental group. Stop when there are 12 cats in the experimental group.

Ⓑ Assign each cat a number, then draw 12 numbers without replacement and put the corresponding cats in the experimental group.

Ⓒ Assign each cat a number, then draw 12 numbers with replacement and put the corresponding cats in the experimental group.

Ⓓ Assign each cat a number, then use a computer program 12 times to choose a random number between 1 and 24 and put the corresponding cats in the experimental group.

Common Core Standards Practice

HSS.IC.B.6

1. Determine if the type of variable of each quantity is Quantitative (Q), Categorical (C), or Neither (N).

	Q	C	N
The color of your eyes	☐	☐	☐
The number of hours teachers work in a week	☐	☐	☐
The number of months in one year	☐	☐	☐
The color of cars owned by people in Destin, Florida	☐	☐	☐

2. A teacher polled her students who scored below the class average on their last math quiz, asking whether they had prepared for the quiz the day before. What is the population of this survey?

   Ⓐ The teacher's students

   Ⓑ Every student who has ever scored below average on a math quiz

   Ⓒ Every student in the school where the teacher works

   Ⓓ The teacher's students who scored below average on their last math quiz

3. Decide if each statement is a Statistic (S) or a Parameter (P).

	S	P
60% of the people in your neighborhood are immigrants.	☐	☐
Based on a sample of 25 students, 30% of High school students travel during spring break.	☐	☐
42% of students in your class scored more than 85 in the last science quiz.	☐	☐

4. Select all that are true about the following question.

   "How many children do families have?"

   ☐ A. The variable is quantitative.

   ☐ B. The variable is categorical.

   ☐ C. The variable is the number of people in families.

   ☐ D. The variable is the number of children families have.

   ☐ E. The variable is the number of children schools have.

5. A survey question is conducted on all single parents in Orlando, Florida. Select whether the type of variable that will result from each survey question is Quantitative (Q) or Categorical (C).

	Q	C
How many children do you have?	☐	☐
Do you get any child support?	☐	☐
What is your monthly income?	☐	☐
Do you have health insurance?	☐	☐
Have you ever been married?	☐	☐

6. A school teacher wants to know which fundraising event is the most popular among his students, so he randomly selects 5 students from each of his 4 classes to participate in a survey.

Part A

How many students are in the sample in this situation?

Part B

What is the population?

Ⓐ All students in the teacher's four classes

Ⓑ The 20 randomly selected students

Ⓒ The entire school

Ⓓ The entire district where the school is located

7. Which of the following statements are statistics? Select all that apply.

☐ A. 30% of the people attending the play are students.

☐ B. 60% of the students in a youth group are seniors.

☐ C. Based on a sample of 40 people leaving a movie theater, 12% would see the movie again.

☐ D. 65% of students in a science class plan on attending college.

☐ E. Based on a sample of 25 people in the cafeteria, 20% students say that apples are their favorite fruit.

8. Which of the following statements is a parameter?

Ⓐ A sample of 40 students finds that 15% of them have never golfed before.

Ⓑ Based on a sample of 50 people at the mall, 60% of people plan on travelling in the next year.

Ⓒ 25% of the students have never golfed before.

Ⓓ 75% of a sample of 20 people said they have read a book in the last year.

9. A survey of 50 students finds that 14% want the school colors to change. Which of the following conclusions most accurately describes the results of the survey?

Ⓐ A low percent of students want the school colors to change.

Ⓑ No students want the school colors to change.

Ⓒ Almost as many students want the school colors to change as do not.

Ⓓ A small number of students want the school colors to change.

Common Core Standards Practice

HSS.MD.B.6, HSS.MD.B.7

1. Mr. Anderson wants to choose 4 students to work on a group project. Each of the 29 students in the class is given a different number from 1 to 29. Which of the following methods will give every student an equal chance of being selected? Select all that apply.

   ☐ **A.** He puts equally sized slips of paper each with a different number from 1 to 29 in a box and withdraws 4 slips of paper.

   ☐ **B.** He rolls a 6-sided die and chooses the student with the number that comes up. Then he rolls the die again, adds 6 to the result, and chooses the student with that number. He repeats the process but with the numbers 12 and 18 added to the result.

   ☐ **C.** He starts with number 1 and flips a coin. If it is heads, the student is selected. He then moves on to the next number and stops when 4 students are selected.

   ☐ **D.** He uses a random number generator to choose 4 different numbers between 1 and 29.

   ☐ **E.** He makes a spinner with 29 equally sized spaces and spins it until he gets 4 different numbers.

2. There are 5 boys and 4 girls in the chess club. They randomly choose 1 boy and 1 girl to get the chess boards from storage. Is this a fair way to choose 2 students? Explain.

   Ⓐ Yes, because they chose randomly.

   Ⓑ Yes, because every girl has an equal chance to be chosen and every boy has an equal chance to be chosen.

   Ⓒ No, because boys have a greater chance of being chosen than girls.

   Ⓓ No, because girls have a greater chance of being chosen than boys.

3. Fran and Eliot are trying to decide what to drink. Fran wants soda and Eliot wants juice. They randomly choose a number between 1 and 100 to help them decide. For each of the methods to choose a drink based on the number, state whether each is fair or not fair.

Method	Fairness
If the number is even, they get soda, if odd, they get juice.	
If the sum of the digits is 10 or less, they get juice, if 11 or more, they get soda.	
If the product of the digits is even, they get juice, if odd, they get soda.	
If the number is between 1 and 50, they get juice, otherwise they get soda.	

4. A disease infects 30% of unvaccinated people and has a 20% chance of causing severe long term health issues or death among those infected. There is a vaccine, so that only 10% of those who are vaccinated get the disease, and only 15% of those people have severe health issues due to the disease. However, 2% of those who get the vaccine have severe health issues from the vaccine. Is it better to get the vaccine or not? Use probability to support your answer.

Ⓐ Get the vaccine; the probability of severe long term health issues without the vaccine is 0.2 and the probability of severe long term health issues with the vaccine is 0.15.

Ⓑ Get the vaccine; the probability of severe long term health issues without the vaccine is 0.2 and the probability of severe long term health issues with the vaccine is 0.17.

Ⓒ Get the vaccine; the probability of severe long term health issues without the vaccine is 0.06 and the probability of severe long term health issues with the vaccine is 0.035.

Ⓓ Get the vaccine; the probability of severe long term health issues without the vaccine is 0.06 and the probability of severe long term health issues with the vaccine is 0.015.

5. Ms. Manning asks her homeroom class of 31 students whether they prefer pizza, burgers, or burritos and whether they prefer juice or water for the end of the year party. Part of a two-way frequency of student preferences is below. What should Ms. Manning serve at the party to make the most students happy about both the food and the beverage?

	Pizza	Burgers	Burritos	Total
Juice		4	5	
Water	6			11
Total				

Ⓐ pizza and juice

Ⓑ pizza and water

Ⓒ burritos and juice

Ⓓ burgers and water

6. Kelly is playing a game of chance. If she bets 3 tokens, she will win 5 tokens when a six-sided die rolls 4 or higher, and 0 tokens otherwise. If she bets 5 tokens, she will get 9 tokens if the die rolls a 5, and 15 tokens if the die rolls a 6. Which bet should she take if she plans to play many times?

She should bet _____ tokens because the expected value is _____ token(s) higher.

enVision® Algebra 2 Common Core Standards Practice Workbook

Name _____

Practice Test Form A

1. The formula for the volume of a sphere is $V = \frac{4}{3}\pi r^3$. Rearrange this formula to solve for the radius.

   _____

2. A car's initial value is $40,000, and it decreases in value 20% each year. Graph the equation that represents the relationship between the year and the value of the car.

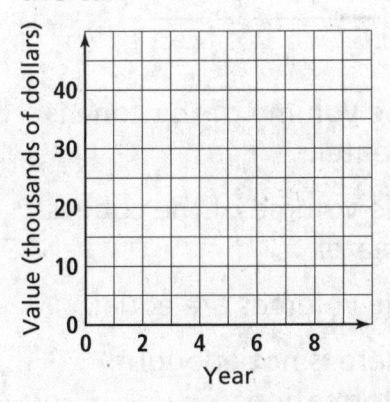

3. Select the value of each expression.

	Value is −1	Value is 1
i^2	☐	☐
$-i^2$	☐	☐
$-i^6$	☐	☐
i^{12}	☐	☐

4. Solve the equation $x^2 + 4x + 5 = 0$.

   _____

5. The angle θ corresponds to the arc length $\frac{2\pi}{3}$ on the unit circle. What is the measure of θ in degrees?

   Ⓐ 30

   Ⓑ 60

   Ⓒ 90

   Ⓓ 120

6. Given the mean μ and standard deviation σ, find the z-score for each data point x. Round to the nearest hundredth if necessary.

	−4.76	−1.5	6.67
$\mu = 17, \sigma = 0.6, x = 21$	☐	☐	☐
$\mu = 3.9, \sigma = 1.2, x = 2.1$	☐	☐	☐
$\mu = 125, \sigma = 4.2, x = 105$	☐	☐	☐

7. Josh randomly chooses 25 students at his school and asks them whether they have a dog as a pet, and 9 students say yes. Based on Josh's data, estimate the proportion of kids at his school that have a dog as a pet.

---

8. Select all the true statements about the function shown in the diagram.

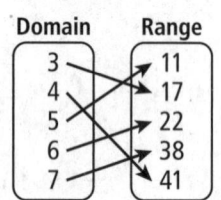

Domain: 3, 4, 5, 6, 7
Range: 11, 17, 22, 38, 41

☐ A. The function is invertible.
☐ B. The function is not invertible.
☐ C. The domain of the inverse function is {11, 17, 22, 38, 41}.
☐ D. The domain of the inverse function is {3, 4, 5, 6, 7}.
☐ E. The domain of the inverse relation is {3, 4, 5, 6, 7, 11, 17, 22, 38, 41}.

9. The volume of a uniform cone with equal height and radius x is $V(x) = \frac{\pi x^3}{3}$. The volume of a cube with side length x is shown in the graph. When $x = 1.2$, which volume is greater?

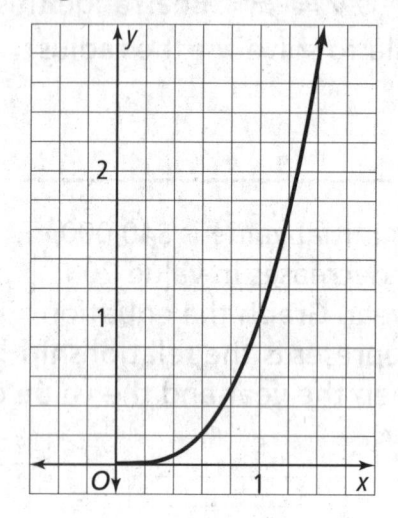

Ⓐ The volume of the cone is greater.
Ⓑ The volume of the cube is greater.
Ⓒ The volumes are equal.
Ⓓ There is not enough information.

---

10. Which expressions are equivalent to $a^4 - 625b^4$? Select all that apply.

☐ A. $(a^2 - 25b^2)^2$
☐ B. $(a - 5b)(a + 5b)^3$
☐ C. $(a - 5b)^2(a + 5b)^2$
☐ D. $(a^2 - 25b^2)(a^2 + 25b^2)$
☐ E. $(a - 5b)(a + 5b)(a^2 + 25b^2)$

11. Graph the functions $f(x) = 2^x - 7$ and $g(x) = \log(x + 5) - 4$. How many solutions are there to the system of $f(x)$ and $g(x)$? Where do the graphs intersect? Round answers to the nearest thousandth if necessary.

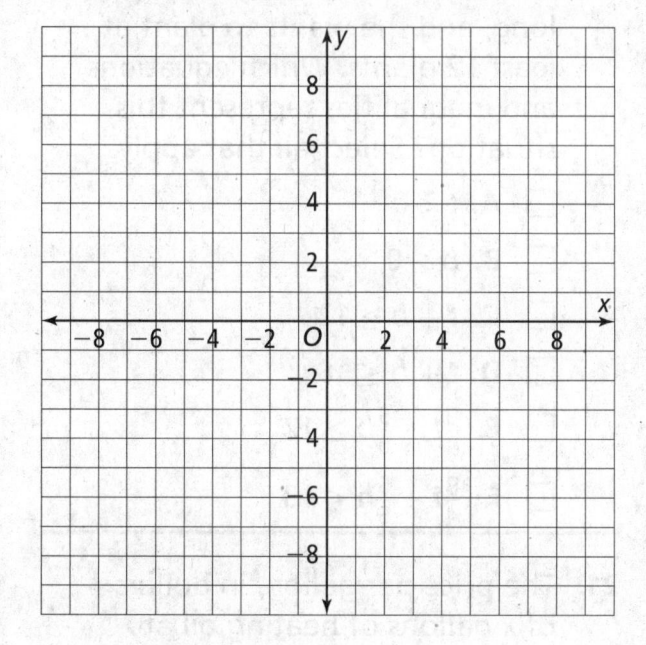

12. Subtract $(2y^2 + 4y - 3x^2 + 3xy + 3)$ from $(4x - 6xy + 4y + 2y^2 + 5)$.

13. Which expression is equivalent to $(x - y - z)^2$?

Ⓐ $x^2 + y^2 + z^2 - 2xy - 2xz - 2yz$
Ⓑ $x^2 + y^2 + z^2 + 2xy - 2xz - 2yz$
Ⓒ $x^2 + y^2 + z^2 - 2xy - 2xz + 2yz$
Ⓓ $x^2 + y^2 + z^2 - 2xy + 2xz - 2yz$

14. A music streaming service has monitored how many downloads, in thousands, a new release received over the past 5 hours.

x (hours)	f(x) (thousands of downloads)
1	2
2	8
3	32
4	128
5	512

☐ **A.** From $x = 1$ to $x = 2$, the average rate of change is 6,000 downloads per hour.

☐ **B.** From $x = 4$ to $x = 5$, the average rate of change is 384 downloads per hour.

☐ **C.** From $x = 4$ to $x = 5$, the average rate of change is 384,000 downloads per hour.

☐ **D.** The download rate increases over time.

☐ **E.** The download rate decreases over time.

15. Determine if each statement about the function $f(x) = -2(x - 5)^2$ is true or false.

	True	False
The vertex is $(-5, 0)$.	☐	☐
The parabola opens down.	☐	☐
The graph is shifted 5 units left from that of $f(x) = x^2$.	☐	☐
The graph is vertically stretched compared to that of $f(x) = x^2$.	☐	☐

16. The formula for continuously compounded interest is $A = Pe^{rt}$. Rearrange this formula to solve for t.

17. What is the product of $(3 - 2i)(3 + 2i)$?

18. Solve $e^{5x} + 2 = 24$. Round your answer to the nearest thousandth.

19. Jamie spins a spinner with spaces numbered 1–5 three times and gets a 5 each time. She thinks that if there is less than a 1% chance that a fair spinner will come up 5 every time with three spins, the spinner is not fair. What is the probability that a fair spinner will come up 5 every time out of three spins, and does Jamie think her spinner is fair?

Ⓐ 20%, fair
Ⓑ 15%, fair
Ⓒ 4%, fair
Ⓓ 0.8%, not fair

20. Lydia wants to plant both tomatoes, t, and beans, b, in her garden. Each tomato plant requires $\frac{9}{4}$ square feet of space, and each bean plant requires $\frac{5}{8}$ square foot. Her garden is a rectangle 3 feet wide and 6 feet long, and she wants to plant at least 12 plants. Which equations and inequalities represent this situation? Select all that apply.

☐ A. $t < 0$
☐ B. $b > 0$
☐ C. $t + b \geq 12$
☐ D. $t + b \leq 18$
☐ E. $\frac{9}{4}t + \frac{5}{8}b \geq 12$
☐ F. $\frac{9}{4}t + \frac{5}{8}b \leq 18$

21. The price per gallon, in dollars, of x gallons of heating oil at WilOil home heating is given by the function

$$f(x) = \begin{cases} 1.5, & 0 \leq x \leq 250 \\ 1.25, & 250 < x \leq 600 \\ 1.15, & 600 < x \leq 1000 \\ 1.00, & x > 1000 \end{cases}$$

Graph the function.

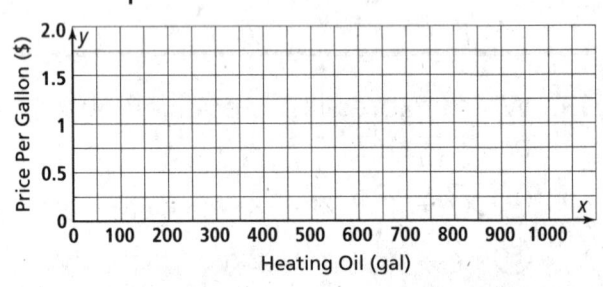

22. Find the inverse of the function $f(x) = (x - 1)^3 + 7$.

23. Jackson randomly selected 10 of the 200 students in his grade and asked them how many siblings they have. The table shows his results.

0	2	1	2	1
4	1	2	0	3

Which is the best estimate of the mean number of siblings all the students in Jackson's grade have?

Ⓐ 1.6
Ⓑ 3.2
Ⓒ 32
Ⓓ Cannot be determined

24. Describe the end behavior of the polynomial function $f(x) = x^2 - 3x^3 + 5x - 3$. Select all that apply.

☐ A. As $x \to -\infty$, $f(x) \to -\infty$.
☐ B. As $x \to -\infty$, $f(x) \to \infty$.
☐ C. As $x \to \infty$, $f(x) \to -\infty$.
☐ D. As $x \to \infty$, $f(x) \to \infty$.
☐ E. As $x \to \infty$, $f(x) \to \infty$.

25. What is $\sin \theta$?

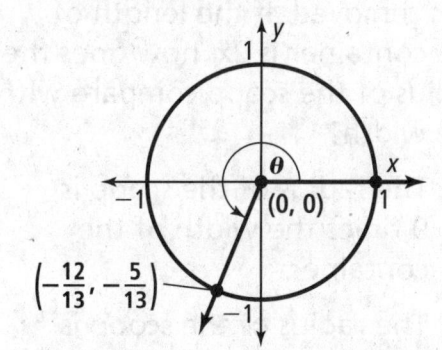

Ⓐ $-\frac{12}{13}$
Ⓑ $-\frac{5}{13}$
Ⓒ $\frac{5}{13}$
Ⓓ $\frac{12}{13}$

26. Select all the expressions that are equivalent to $\sqrt[4]{x^6}$.

☐ A. $x^{\frac{4}{6}}$
☐ B. $x^{\frac{6}{4}}$
☐ C. $x^{1.5}$
☐ D. $\sqrt{x^3}$
☐ E. $\sqrt[3]{x^2}$

27. Martin graphed a function $c(x)$ that shows the cost for a streaming device that charges him monthly only if he uses it that month. Which domain is most appropriate to use to determine the cost in the first year?

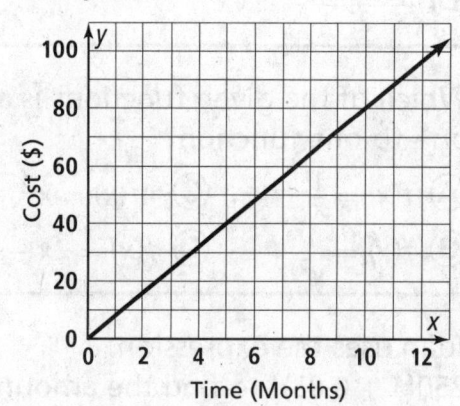

Ⓐ real numbers less than or equal to 12
Ⓑ whole numbers less than or equal to 12
Ⓒ positive rational numbers less than or equal to 12
Ⓓ positive irrational numbers less than or equal to 12

28. Given $\sin \theta = \frac{3}{5}$ and θ is in Quadrant II, what is $\cos \theta$?

Ⓐ $-\frac{4}{5}$
Ⓑ $-\frac{3}{5}$
Ⓒ $\frac{3}{5}$
Ⓓ $\frac{4}{5}$

29. Let $f(x) = 3x + 7$ and $g(x) = (x - 4)^2$. Find $(f + g)(x)$, $(g - f)(x)$, and $g(f(x))$.

	$(f + g)(x)$	$(g - f)(x)$	$g(f(x))$
$x^2 - 5x + 23$	☐	☐	☐
$x^2 - 11x + 9$	☐	☐	☐
$9x^2 + 18x + 9$	☐	☐	☐

30. Which are the solutions to the equation $x^2 + 2x + 9 = 0$?
    Ⓐ $\frac{-3 \pm i3\sqrt{3}}{2}$
    Ⓑ $\frac{-3 \pm 3\sqrt{5}}{2}$
    Ⓒ $\frac{3 \pm i3\sqrt{3}}{2}$
    Ⓓ $\frac{3 \pm 3\sqrt{5}}{2}$

31. Which of the given functions is a one-to-one function?
    Ⓐ $f(x) = \frac{1}{x}$
    Ⓑ $f(x) = \frac{1}{x^2}$
    Ⓒ $4f(x) = x^2$
    Ⓓ $f(x) = 2x - x^2$

32. Juan uses the expression $250(1 + 0.03)^t$ to find the amount of money he will have in his bank account after t years. Select all the statements that are true.
    ☐ A. 250 represents Juan's initial deposit of $250.
    ☐ B. 250 represents the amount of money Juan will have after t years.
    ☐ C. Juan's account earns 1% interest.
    ☐ D. Juan's account earns 3% interest.
    ☐ E. Juan's account earns 30% interest.

33. Which expression equals $\frac{6x^3 - 2x^2 + 3x - 4}{x + 2}$?
    Ⓐ $6x^2 - 2$
    Ⓑ $6x^2 - 2x + 3$
    Ⓒ $6x^2 - 14x + 31 - \frac{66}{x + 2}$
    Ⓓ $6x^2 - 14x + 31 + \frac{58}{x + 2}$

34. Shelby is packing a gift inside of a box to send to her friend. The gift is a cube with side length 7 inches. She has 100 in.^{3} of packing peanuts to pack around the gift. Write an equation that relates x, the volume of the box, with the side length of the gift.

35. Using the equation you wrote in Item 34, find the volume of the box, in cubic inches.

36. The expression $2x(x)(x) - \frac{4\pi}{81}x^3$ represents the volume of ice cream left in a rectangular prism-shaped container after a spherical scoop was removed. If the length of the container is $2x$, how does the radius of the scoop compare with the width?
    Ⓐ The radius of the scoop is 9 times the width of the container.
    Ⓑ The radius of the scoop is 3 times the width of the container.
    Ⓒ The radius of the scoop is $\frac{1}{9}$ the width of the container.
    Ⓓ The radius of the scoop is $\frac{1}{3}$ the width of the container.

37. Multiply $(3ab - 2)(2a^2 + 2ab - 3b^2)$.

Ⓐ $6a^3b + 6a^2b^2 + 9ab^3 - 4a^2 - 4ab + 6b^2$

Ⓑ $6a^3b + 6ab^2 - 9a^2b^3 - 4a^2 + 4ab + 6b^2$

Ⓒ $6a^3b + 4a^3b^2 - 9ab^3 - 4a^2 - 4ab + 6b^2$

Ⓓ $6a^3b + 6a^2b^2 - 9ab^3 - 4a^2 - 4ab + 6b^2$

38. Select all the zeros of $x^3 - 9x^2 + 20x$.

☐ A. −5
☐ B. −4
☐ C. 0
☐ D. 4
☐ E. 5

39. A company wants to know if their new drug works better than the current ones. What kind of study should they do?

Ⓐ experiment
Ⓑ observational study
Ⓒ sample survey
Ⓓ study group

40. Determine if $(x + 4)$ is a factor of $p(x) = x^3 - 2x^2 - 19x + 20$. If so, write $p(x)$ as a product of prime factors.

Ⓐ yes; $(x + 4)(x^2 + 4x + 5)$
Ⓑ yes; $(x - 1)(x + 4)(x - 5)$
Ⓒ yes; $(x + 4)(x + 1)(x + 5)$
Ⓓ no

41. Match each equation with its solution.

Equation	−15.31	−0.54	52.5
$\log(2x - 5) = 2$	☐	☐	☐
$2\log(5x + 3) = -1$	☐	☐	☐
$\log(1 - 2x) = 1.5$	☐	☐	☐

42. Which expression is a factor of $x^3 + 2x^2 - 5x - 6$?

Ⓐ $x - 1$
Ⓑ $x + 1$
Ⓒ $x + 2$
Ⓓ $x - 3$

43. Find the average rate of change of $f(x) = \log(x + 3) - 2$ change of over the interval [7, 97].

44. Select all the solutions of the equation of $x^3 - 3x^2 - 3x + 1 = 0$.

☐ A. -1
☐ B. 1
☐ C. $2 + \sqrt{3}$
☐ D. $-2 + \sqrt{3}$
☐ E. $2 - \sqrt{3}$

45. Chris made a few mistakes while finding the real solutions of the equation $\frac{1}{4}\sqrt[3]{x + 10x^2} = x$. Check the steps below to determine which step is not mathematically correct.

Step 1: Multiply both sides by 4 to get $\sqrt[3]{x + 10x^2} = 4x$.

Step 2: Raise to the power 3 $x + 10x^2 = 4x$.

Step 3: Simplify the resulting equation $10x^2 - 3x = 0$.

Step 4: Solve the resulting equation to get $x = 0$ or $x = 0.3$.

Ⓐ Step 1
Ⓑ Step 2
Ⓒ Step 3
Ⓓ Step 4

46. A sandwich shop needs to sell at least $1,250 worth of sandwiches and drinks each day to cover its costs. Each sandwich costs $9 and each drink costs $3. The shop has never sold more than 120 sandwiches in a day. Let the number of sandwiches sold be s and the number of drinks sold be d. Which set of inequalities models this situation?

Ⓐ $s + d \geq 1{,}250$
$s \geq 0$
$120 \geq d \geq 0$

Ⓑ $3s + 9d \geq 1{,}250$
$120 \geq s \geq 0$
$d \geq 0$

Ⓒ $s + d > 1{,}250$
$s \geq 0$
$120 \geq d \geq 0$

Ⓓ $3.5x + 2.75y > 1{,}250$
$120 \geq s \geq 0$
$d \geq 0$

47. What is the leading coefficient of the following polynomial?

$P(x) = 5x^2 - 2x^3 + 11x - 6$

48. The profit a bicycle manufacturer makes from building and selling n bicycles is represented by the function $P(n) = -2n^2 + 260n - 5{,}000$. Which is the appropriate domain for this function?

Ⓐ all integers
Ⓑ all real numbers
Ⓒ positive integers
Ⓓ positive real numbers

49. A university randomly selects 500 of its 8,000 students to survey their opinions on class availability. What is the size of the sample?

Ⓐ 8,000

Ⓑ 7,500

Ⓒ 500

Ⓓ 6.3

50. Consider the functions $f(x) = |-3x| - 4$ and $g(x) = \frac{x^2}{3} + 1$. In which ranges do the x-values of the solutions to the equation $f(x) = g(x)$ fall? Select all that apply.

☐ A. [−4, −3]

☐ B. [−3, −2]

☐ C. [−2, −1]

☐ D. [−1, 1]

☐ E. [1, 2]

☐ F. [2, 3]

☐ G. [3, 4]

51. What is the equation of a parabola that passes through the points (−1, 4), (0, 5), and (2, −11)?

Ⓐ $y = -3x^2 + 2x + 5$

Ⓑ $y = -2x^2 - 3x + 5$

Ⓒ $y = -3x^2 - 2x + 5$

Ⓓ $y = -2x^2 + 3x + 5$

52. What is cos θ?

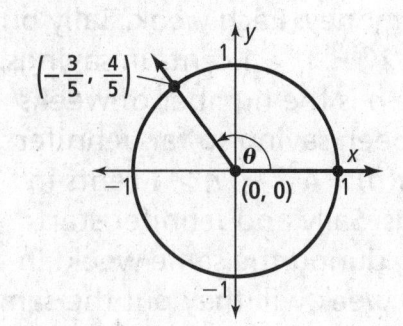

Ⓐ $-\frac{4}{5}$

Ⓑ $-\frac{3}{5}$

Ⓒ $\frac{3}{5}$

Ⓓ $\frac{4}{5}$

53. Which expression is equivalent to $3i(4 - 2i)$?

Ⓐ $-6 - 12i$

Ⓑ $-6 + 12i$

Ⓒ $6 - 12i$

Ⓓ $6 + 12i$

54. The expression $x(2x)(x - 5)$ could represent which of the following?

Ⓐ the volume of a box whose length is twice its width and whose height is 5 units less than its width

Ⓑ the volume of a box whose length is twice its width and whose height is 5 units less than its length

Ⓒ the volume of a box whose length is two more than its width and whose height is 5 units less than its width

Ⓓ the volume of a box whose length is twice its width and whose height is 5 units more than its width

55. Sally and Jennifer want to save some money. Each week, Sally puts $f(n) = 2^{n+9}$; $n \geq 1$ cents in savings, where n is the number of weeks she's been saving so far. Jennifer puts $g(n) = 4^{2n-3}$; $n \geq 1$ cents in savings. Sally and Jennifer start saving during the same week. In which week will they put the same amount of money in their savings?

56. Sandra learns a new swimming technique and records her times using the new technique and the old technique in a table. How do her times between the two techniques compare?

| Old Technique (s) | 31.8 | 29.3 | 31.5 | 26.2 | 35.9 |
| New Technique (s) | 28.4 | 30 | 25.8 | 24.5 | 32.9 |

Ⓐ The new technique is faster on average by 2.62 seconds.

Ⓑ The new technique is slower on average by 2.62 seconds.

Ⓒ The new technique is faster on average by 8.47 seconds.

Ⓓ The new technique is slower on average by 8.47 seconds.

57. Tomas has determined that the local temperature in degrees Fahrenheit of an area can be modeled by a cosine function with an amplitude of 8, a midline of 72, and a period of 24 hours. Which function models the temperature?

Ⓐ $y = 8 \cos \frac{\pi x}{24} + 72$

Ⓑ $y = 72 \cos \frac{\pi x}{24} + 8$

Ⓒ $y = 8 \cos \frac{\pi x}{12} + 72$

Ⓓ $y = 72 \cos \frac{\pi x}{12} + 8$

58. The edge length of a cube is represented by the expression $2x - 3$. Which expression represents the volume of the cube?

Ⓐ $4x^2 + 9$

Ⓑ $4x^2 - 12x + 9$

Ⓒ $8x^3 - 27$

Ⓓ $8x^3 - 36x^2 + 54x - 27$

59. The student council is doing research to find out how to improve school lunches. Select all the statements that are parameters.

☐ A. 77% of students at the school buy their lunch.

☐ B. Of students who eat during the first lunch period, 27% bring their lunch.

☐ C. 1 out of 2 survey respondents would like a salad bar in the cafeteria.

☐ D. Half of the seniors bring their lunch.

☐ E. More students buy lunch on Fridays than on Mondays.

60. The graph of an exponential model in the form $f(x) = a \cdot b^x$ passes through the points (1, 3) and (0, 2). Select the points that are also on the graph.

☐ A. (3, 6)

☐ B. (−1, −1)

☐ C. (−3, −0.5)

☐ D. (2, 4.5)

☐ E. (3, 6.75)

Name _____

Practice Test Form B

1. The formula for the surface area of a sphere is $V = 4\pi r^2$. Rearrange this formula to solve for the radius.

2. A car's initial value is $20,000, and it decreases in value 15% each year. Graph the equation that represents the relationship between the year and the value of the car.

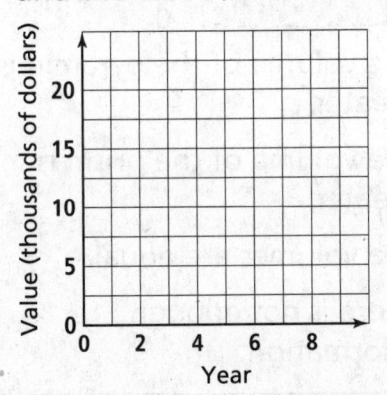

3. Select the value of each expression.

	Value is −1	Value is 1
i^3	❑	❑
i^6	❑	❑
$-i^{10}$	❑	❑
$-i^{48}$	❑	❑

4. Solve the equation $x^2 - 2x + 2 = 0$.

5. The angle θ corresponds to the arc length $\frac{5\pi}{6}$ on the unit circle. What is the measure of θ in degrees?
   - Ⓐ 15
   - Ⓑ 75
   - Ⓒ 150
   - Ⓓ 300

6. Given the mean μ and standard deviation σ, find the z-score for each data point x. Round to the nearest hundredth if necessary.

	−1.12	1.19	2.77
$\mu = 21.4, \sigma = 6.3, x = 28.9$	❑	❑	❑
$\mu = 42, \sigma = 3, x = 12.5$	❑	❑	❑
$\mu = 8, \sigma = 4.1, x = 3.4$	❑	❑	❑

7. Patricia randomly chooses 25 students at her school and asks them whether they have a pet, and 17 students say yes. Based on Patricia's data, estimate the proportion of kids at her school that have a pet.

---

8. Select all the true statements about the function shown in the diagram.

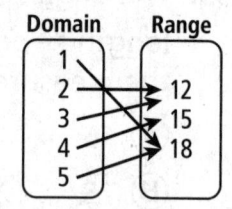

   Domain: 1, 2, 3, 4, 5 → Range: 12, 15, 18

   ☐ A. The function is invertible.

   ☐ B. The function is not invertible.

   ☐ C. The domain of the inverse function is {12, 15, 18}.

   ☐ D. The domain of the inverse function is {1, 2, 3, 4, 5}.

   ☐ E. The domain of the inverse relation is {12, 15, 18}.

---

9. The volume of a square-based pyramid with equal height and base side lengths x is $V(x) = \frac{x^3}{3}$. The volume of a particular rectangular prism with height x is shown in the graph. When $x = 0.5$, which volume is greater?

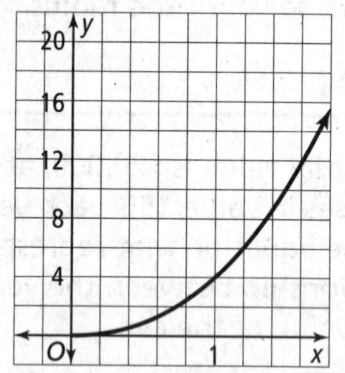

   Ⓐ The volume of the pyramid is greater.

   Ⓑ The volume of the prism is greater.

   Ⓒ The volumes are equal.

   Ⓓ There is not enough information.

---

10. Which expressions are equivalent to $x^4 - 256y^8$? Select all that apply.

    ☐ A. $(x^2 - 16y^4)^2$

    ☐ B. $(x - 4y^2)(x + 4y^2)^3$

    ☐ C. $(x + 4y^2)^2(x + 4y^2)^2$

    ☐ D. $(x^2 - 16y^4)(x^2 + 16y^4)$

    ☐ E. $(x - 4y^2)(x + 4y^2)(x^2 + 16y^4)$

11. Graph the functions $f(x) = 0.5^x + 1$ and $g(x) = 2 - \dfrac{9}{(x^2 + 3)}$. How many solutions are there to the system of $f(x)$ and $g(x)$? Where do the graphs intersect? Round answers to the nearest thousandth if necessary.

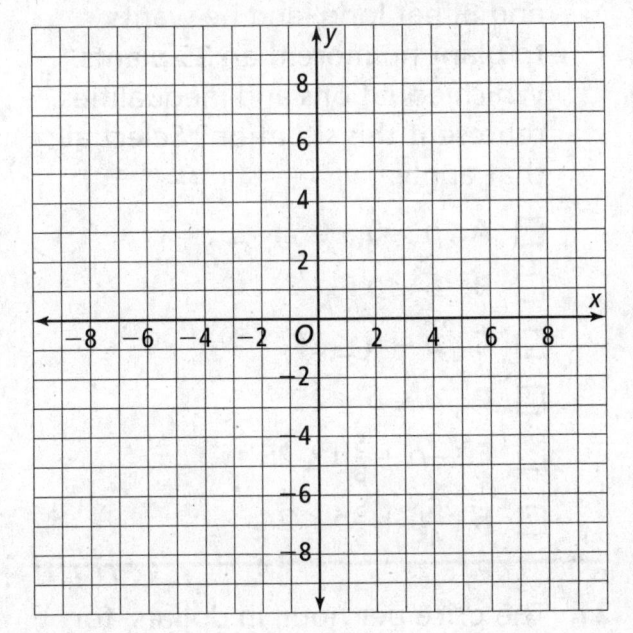

12. Subtract $(3a^2 - b + 2b^2 + ab - 5)$ from $(5a + 8ab - 3b + 2b^2 + 2)$.

13. Which expression is equivalent to $(x - y + z)^2$?

Ⓐ $x^2 + y^2 + z^2 - 2xy - 2xz - 2yz$
Ⓑ $x^2 + y^2 + z^2 + 2xy - 2xz - 2yz$
Ⓒ $x^2 + y^2 + z^2 - 2xy - 2xz + 2yz$
Ⓓ $x^2 + y^2 + z^2 - 2xy + 2xz - 2yz$

14. A hospital monitored the growth of bacteria cells by estimating the number of cells, in hundreds, over a 4-hour period.

x (hours)	f(x) (hundreds of cells)
0	4
1	12
2	36
3	108
4	324

☐ A. From $x = 0$ to $x = 2$, the average rate of change is 1600 cells per hour.

☐ B. From $x = 2$ to $x = 4$, the average rate of change is 14,400 cells per hour.

☐ C. From $x = 2$ to $x = 4$, the average rate of change is 7200 cells per hour.

☐ D. The growth rate increases over time.

☐ E. The growth rate decreases over time.

15. Determine if each statement about the function $f(x) = -(x + 3)^2$ is true or false.

	True	False
The vertex is (3, 0).	☐	☐
The parabola opens down.	☐	☐
The graph is shifted 3 units left from that of $f(x) = x^2$.	☐	☐
The graph is vertically stretched compared to that of $f(x) = x^2$.	☐	☐

16. The formula for quarterly compounded interest is $A = P\left(1 + \frac{r}{4}\right)^{4t}$. Rearrange this formula to solve for t.

17. What is the product of $(4 + 3i)(1 + i)$?

18. Solve $e^{5x} + 2 = 24$. Round your answer to the nearest thousandth.

19. Maria spins a spinner with spaces numbered 1–4 four times and gets a 4 each time. She thinks that if there is less than a 1% chance that a fair spinner will come up 4 every time with four spins, the spinner is not fair. What is the probability that a fair spinner will come up 4 every time out of four spins, and does Maria think her spinner is fair?

Ⓐ 0.4%, not fair
Ⓑ 1.6%, fair
Ⓒ 6.3%, fair
Ⓓ 16%, fair

20. Will wants to plant both peppers, p, and beans, b, in his garden. Each pepper plant requires $\frac{5}{4}$ square feet of space, and each bean plant requires $\frac{5}{8}$ square foot. His garden is a rectangle 3 feet wide and 8 feet long, and he wants to plant no more than 25 plants. Which equations and inequalities represent this situation? Select all that apply.

☐ A. $p > 0$
☐ B. $b < 0$
☐ C. $p + b \leq 24$
☐ D. $p + b \leq 25$
☐ E. $\frac{5}{4}p + \frac{5}{8}b \leq 25$
☐ F. $\frac{5}{4}p + \frac{5}{8}b \leq 24$

21. The price per hour, in dollars, for using an event space for x hours in a month is given by the function
$$f(x) = \begin{cases} 22, & 0 \leq x \leq 20 \\ 18, & 20 < x \leq 75 \\ 15, & 75 < x \leq 100 \\ 13, & x > 100 \end{cases}$$
Graph the function.

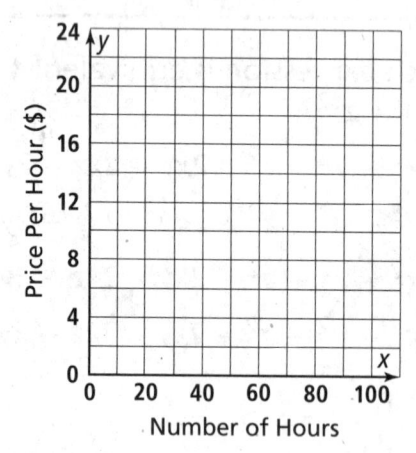

22. Find the inverse of the function $f^{-1}(x) = \frac{1}{2}\sqrt[3]{x+4} + 15$.

_____

23. Jackson randomly selected 10 of the 150 students in his grade and asked them how many other states they have lived in. The table shows his results.

0	1	7	0	3
0	3	0	2	2

Which is the best estimate of the mean number of siblings all the students in Jackson's grade have?

Ⓐ 1.8

Ⓑ 2.7

Ⓒ 27

Ⓓ Cannot be determined

_____

24. Describe the end behavior of the polynomial function
$f(x) = 2x^2 + 3x^3 + 4x + 1$.
Select all that apply.

☐ A. As $x \to -\infty$, $f(x) \to -\infty$.

☐ B. As $x \to -\infty$, $f(x) \to \infty$.

☐ C. As $x \to \infty$, $f(x) \to -\infty$.

☐ D. As $x \to \infty$, $f(x) \to \infty$.

☐ E. As $x \to \infty$, $f(x) \to \infty$.

25. What is $\cos \theta$?

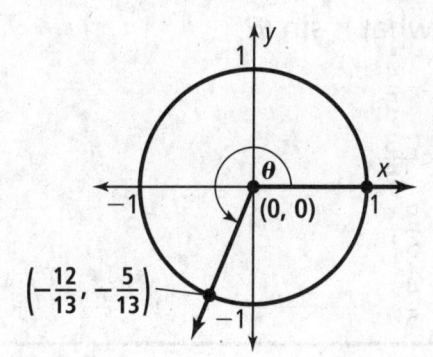

Ⓐ $-\frac{12}{13}$ Ⓒ $\frac{5}{13}$

Ⓑ $-\frac{5}{13}$ Ⓓ $\frac{12}{13}$

_____

26. Select all the expressions that are equivalent to $x^{\frac{5}{3}}$.

☐ A. $\left(x^{\frac{1}{9}}\right)^{15}$

☐ B. $\sqrt{x^5}$

☐ C. x^{15}

☐ D. $\sqrt[5]{x^3}$

☐ E. $\sqrt[3]{x^5}$

_____

27. The function $p(x)$ models the price of cookies at a bakery. Which domain is most appropriate to use in the model of this situation?

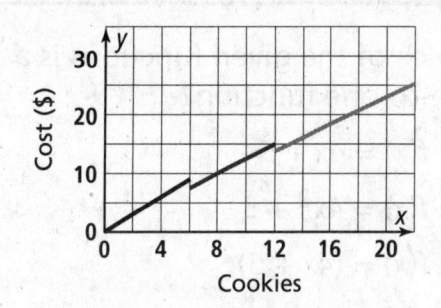

Ⓐ whole numbers

Ⓑ positive real numbers

Ⓒ positive rational numbers

Ⓓ positive irrational numbers

28. Given $\cos \theta = \frac{4}{5}$ and θ is in Quadrant IV, what is $\sin \theta$?

   Ⓐ $-\frac{4}{5}$

   Ⓑ $-\frac{3}{5}$

   Ⓒ $\frac{3}{5}$

   Ⓓ $\frac{4}{5}$

29. Let $f(x) = 5x - 2$ and $g(x) = (x + 1)^2$. Find $(g + f)(x)$, $(f - g)(x)$, and $f(g(x))$.

	$(g + f)(x)$	$(f - g)(x)$	$f(g(x))$
$-x^2 + 3x - 3$	☐	☐	☐
$x^2 + 7x - 1$	☐	☐	☐
$5x^2 + 10x + 3$	☐	☐	☐

30. Which are the solutions to the equation $x^2 - 5x + 11 = 0$?

   Ⓐ $\frac{-5 \pm i\sqrt{19}}{2}$

   Ⓑ $\frac{-5 \pm \sqrt{69}}{2}$

   Ⓒ $\frac{5 \pm i\sqrt{19}}{2}$

   Ⓓ $\frac{5 \pm \sqrt{69}}{2}$

31. Which of the given functions is a one-to-one function?

   Ⓐ $f(x) = 4x + 5$

   Ⓑ $f(x) = 4x^2 + 5$

   Ⓒ $f(x) = (4x + 5)^2$

   Ⓓ $f(x) = \frac{1}{4x^2} + 5$

32. Kenan uses the expression $(36 - 2x)(24 - 2x)$ to find the area of a rectangular canvas after cutting out an equal-size square from each corner. Select all the statements that are true.

   ☐ A. The original length of the canvas was 36.

   ☐ B. The original width of the canvas was 24.

   ☐ C. The side length of the square Kenan cut out is x.

   ☐ D. The side length of the square Kenan cut out is $2x$.

   ☐ E. The side length of the square Kenan cut out is $\frac{1}{2}x$.

33. Which expression equals $\frac{5x^3 + 6x^2 - 4x + 6}{x + 1}$?

   Ⓐ $5x^2 + 6$

   Ⓑ $5x^2 + 6x - 4$

   Ⓒ $5x^2 + x - 5 + \frac{1}{x + 1}$

   Ⓓ $5x^2 + x - 5 + \frac{11}{x + 1}$

34. Jamison is framing a square picture that has side length 8 inches. He knows that the area of the mat that surrounds the picture will be 80 in.². Write an equation that relates x, the total area of the picture and mat, with the side length of the picture.

35. Using the equation you wrote in Item 34, find the total area of the picture and mat, in square inches.

___

36. The expression $64x^3 - \frac{4}{3}\pi x^3$ represents the volume of ice cream left in a cube-shaped container after a spherical scoop was removed. How does side length of the container compare with the radius of the scoop?

Ⓐ The side length of the container is 4 times the radius of the scoop.

Ⓑ The side length of the container is 2 times the radius of the scoop.

Ⓒ The side length of the container is $\frac{1}{2}$ the radius of the scoop.

Ⓓ The side length of the container is $\frac{1}{4}$ the radius of the scoop.

___

37. Multiply $(4pq + 3)(p^2 - 5q^2 + 1)$.

Ⓐ $20p^3q + 4pq^3 + 3p^2 - 15q^2 + 3$

Ⓑ $4p^3q - 20pq^3 + 3p^2 + 4pq - 15q^2 + 3$

Ⓒ $4p^3q + 8pq^3 - 12p^2q^2 + 4pq + 3$

Ⓓ $4p^3q + 3pq^3 - 15p^2q - 20pq^2 + pq + 3$

___

38. Select all the zeros of $x^3 - 16x$.

☐ A. -58

☐ B. -4

☐ C. 0

☐ D. 4

☐ E. 8

___

39. A company wants to know if people with a certain health condition want a new medication or are happy the current ones. What kind of study should they do?

Ⓐ experiment

Ⓑ observational study

Ⓒ sample survey

Ⓓ study group

___

40. Determine if $(x - 3)$ is a factor of $p(x) = 4x^3 - 20x^2 + 19x + 15$. If so, write $p(x)$ as a product of prime factors.

Ⓐ yes; $(x - 3)(4x^2 + 4x - 10)$

Ⓑ yes; $(x - 3)(4x^2 - 8x - 5)$

Ⓒ yes; $(x - 3)(2x + 1)(2x - 5)$

Ⓓ no

___

41. Match each equation with its solution.

	-7.16	-1.45	15
$3 \log (x - 5) = 3$	☐	☐	☐
$\log (2x + 3) = -1$	☐	☐	☐
$\log (3 - 4x) = 1.5$	☐	☐	☐

42. Which expression is a factor of $x^3 - 2x^2 - 9x + 18$?

   Ⓐ $x - 3$
   Ⓑ $x + 2$
   Ⓒ $x + 6$
   Ⓓ $x - 6$

43. Find the average rate of change of $f(x) = 3\sqrt{x - 2}$ change of over the interval [6, 11]

44. Select all the solutions of the equation of $x^3 + 6x^2 - 5x - 22 = 0$.

   ☐ A. -11
   ☐ B. 2
   ☐ C. $-4 + \sqrt{5}$
   ☐ D. $4 + \sqrt{5}$
   ☐ E. $-4 - \sqrt{5}$

45. Anton made a few mistakes while finding the real solutions of the equation $2\sqrt[3]{10x + 2x^2} = x$. Check the steps below to determine which step is not mathematically correct.

   Step 1: Divide both sides by 2 to get $\sqrt[3]{10x + 2x^2} = \frac{x}{2}$.

   Step 2: Raise to the power 3: $10x + 2x^2 = \frac{x^3}{8}$.

   Step 3: Simplify the resulting equation: $x^3 - 2x^2 - 10x = 0$.

   Step 4: Solve the resulting equation to get $x = 0$ or $x \approx -2.3$.

   Ⓐ Step 1
   Ⓑ Step 2
   Ⓒ Step 3
   Ⓓ Step 4

46. Anita has $60 to spend at a carnival. Each ride ticket costs $3.50, and each game ticket costs $2.75. She wants to go on at least 8 rides and play at least 6 games. Let x be the number of rides and y be the number of games. Which set of inequalities models this situation?

   Ⓐ $3.5x + 2.75y < 60$
      $x \leq 8$
      $y \leq 6$

   Ⓑ $3.5x + 2.75y < 60$
      $x \geq 8$
      $y \geq 6$

   Ⓒ $3.5x + 2.75y \leq 60$
      $x \leq 8$
      $y \leq 6$

   Ⓓ $3.5x + 2.75y \leq 60$
      $x \geq 8$
      $y \geq 6$

47. What is the leading coefficient of the following polynomial?
   $P(x) = 12x^2 - 8x^3 + 3 - x$

48. The temperature in degrees Celsius h hours after noon is modeled by the function $T(h) = -\frac{1}{3}h^2 + 2n + 4$. Which is the appropriate domain for this function?

   Ⓐ all integers
   Ⓑ all real numbers
   Ⓒ positive integers
   Ⓓ positive real numbers

49. A university randomly selects 600 of its 9,000 students to survey their opinions on class availability. What is the size of the sample?

Ⓐ 6.6
Ⓑ 600
Ⓒ 8,400
Ⓓ 9,000

50. Consider the functions $f(x) = \frac{1}{2}(3)^x$ and $g(x) = -x^2 + 12$. In which ranges do the x-values of the solutions to the equation $f(x) = g(x)$ fall? Select all that apply.

☐ A. [−4, −3]
☐ B. [−3, −2]
☐ C. [−2, −1]
☐ D. [−1, 1]
☐ E. [1, 2]
☐ F. [2, 3]
☐ G. [3, 4]

51. What is the equation of a parabola that passes through the points (−2, 6), (0, −4), and (1, 0)?

Ⓐ $y = -x^2 - x - 4$
Ⓑ $y = x^2 + 0.5x - 4$
Ⓒ $y = -3x^2 + x + 4$
Ⓓ $y = 3x^2 + x - 4$

52. What is tan θ?

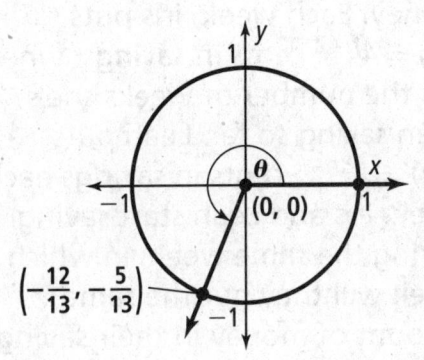

Ⓐ $-\frac{12}{13}$
Ⓑ $\frac{5}{13}$
Ⓒ $\frac{5}{12}$
Ⓓ $\frac{12}{13}$

53. Which expression is equivalent to $-4i(2 + 3i)$?

Ⓐ $12 + 8i$
Ⓑ $12 - 8i$
Ⓒ $-12 + 8i$
Ⓓ $-12 - 8i$

54. The expression $(x - 4)(x - 5)$ could represent which of the following?

Ⓐ the remaining area of a square with side length x after 4 units were cut from one side and 5 units were cut from an adjacent side

Ⓑ the area of a rectangle with length 5 units and width 4 units

Ⓒ the volume of a box whose length is 4 less than its width and whose height is 5 units less than its width

Ⓓ the remaining perimeter of a square with side length x after 4 units were cut from one side and 5 units were cut from an adjacent side

55. Iris and Leah want to save some money. Each week, Iris puts $f(n) = 4^{n+2}$ cents in savings, where n is the number of weeks she's been saving so far. Leah puts $g(n) = 2^{3n-1}$ cents in savings each week. Iris and Leah start saving during the same week. In which week will they put the same amount of money in their savings?

56. Charlotte learns a new swimming technique and records her times using the new technique and the old technique in a table. How do her times between the two techniques compare?

| Old Technique (s) | 32.1 | 31.2 | 35.6 | 30.2 | 35.8 |
| New Technique (s) | 28.2 | 27.1 | 27.5 | 33.1 | 34.1 |

Ⓐ The new technique is faster on average by 9.04 seconds.

Ⓑ The new technique is slower on average by 9.04 seconds.

Ⓒ The new technique is faster on average by 2.98 seconds.

Ⓓ The new technique is slower on average by 2.98 seconds.

57. Eliot has determined that the local temperature in degrees Fahrenheit of an area can be modeled by a cosine function with an amplitude of 7, a midline of 69, and a period of 24 hours. Which function models the temperature?

Ⓐ $y = 69 \cos \frac{\pi x}{24} + 7$

Ⓑ $y = 7 \cos \frac{\pi x}{24} + 69$

Ⓒ $y = 69 \cos \frac{\pi x}{12} + 7$

Ⓓ $y = 7 \cos \frac{\pi x}{12} + 69$

58. The edge length of a cube is represented by the expression $3x + 2$. Which expression represents the volume of the cube?

Ⓐ $9x^2 + 4$

Ⓑ $27x^3 + 8$

Ⓒ $9x^2 + 12x + 4$

Ⓓ $27x^3 + 54x^2 + 36x + 8$

59. The student council is doing research to find out how to improve school lunches. Select all the statements that are statistics.

☐ A. Of students who eat during the first lunch period, 14% bring their lunch.

☐ B. 1 out of 3 students at the school bring their lunch.

☐ C. 15% of survey respondents would like a wider variety of foods in the cafeteria.

☐ D. A fifth of the sophomores bring their lunch.

☐ E. More students buy lunch on Thursdays than on Tuesdays.

60. The graph of an exponential model in the form $f(x) = a \cdot b^x$ passes through the points (1, 6) and (0, 1.5). Select the points that are also on the graph.

☐ A. (2, 24)

☐ B. (−1, 1)

☐ C. (−3, 0.1)

☐ D. (3, 21)

☐ E. (−1, 0.375)

High School Mathematics Reference Sheet

1 inch = 2.54 centimeters
1 mile = 5280 feet
1 mile = 1760 yards
1 mile = 1.609 kilometers
1 kilometer = 0.62 mile
1 meter = 39.37 inches

1 pound = 16 ounces
1 pound = 0.454 kilograms
1 kilogram = 2.2 pounds
1 ton = 2000 pounds

1 cup = 8 fluid ounces
1 pint = 2 cups
1 quart = 2 pints
1 gallon = 4 quarts
1 gallon = 3.785 liters
1 liter = 0.264 gallons
1 liter = 1000 cubic centimeters

Exponential Growth: $y = a(1 + r)^t$

Exponential Decay: $y = a(1 - r)^t$

Compound Interest: $A = P\left(1 + \frac{r}{n}\right)^{nt}$

Continually Compounding Interest: $A = Pe^{rt}$

Arithmetic Sequence: $a_n = a_1 + (n - 1)d$

Geometric Sequence: $a_n = a_1(r)^{n-1}$

Finite Geometric Series:
$S_n = a_1 \frac{(1 - r^n)}{1} - r$

Degrees: 1 degree = $\frac{\pi}{180}$ radians

Radians: 1 radian = $\frac{180}{\pi}$ degrees